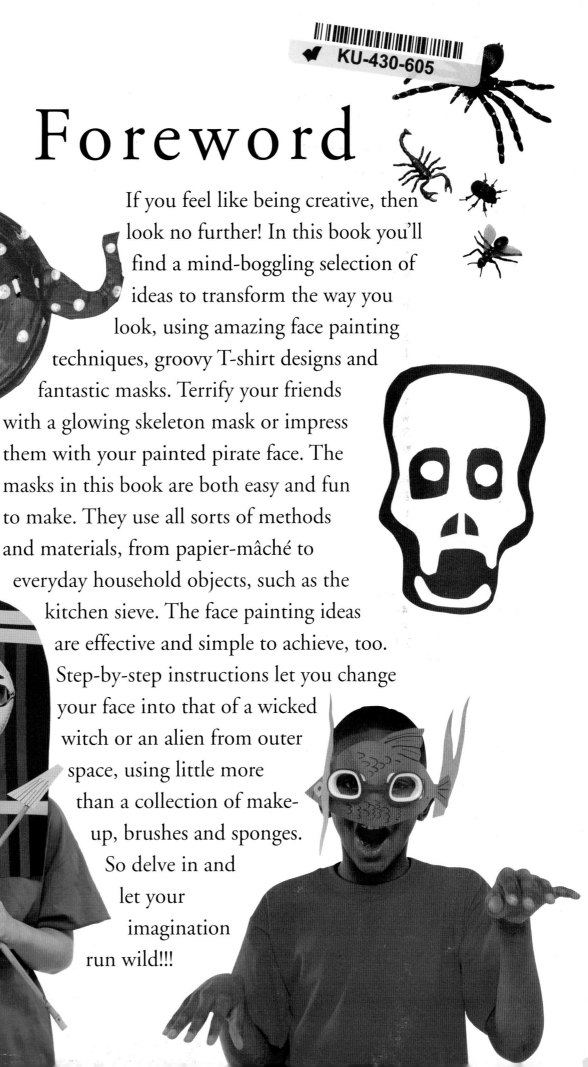

Foreword

If you feel like being creative, then look no further! In this book you'll find a mind-boggling selection of ideas to transform the way you look, using amazing face painting techniques, groovy T-shirt designs and fantastic masks. Terrify your friends with a glowing skeleton mask or impress them with your painted pirate face. The masks in this book are both easy and fun to make. They use all sorts of methods and materials, from papier-mâché to everyday household objects, such as the kitchen sieve. The face painting ideas are effective and simple to achieve, too. Step-by-step instructions let you change your face into that of a wicked witch or an alien from outer space, using little more than a collection of make-up, brushes and sponges. So delve in and let your imagination run wild!!!

Contents

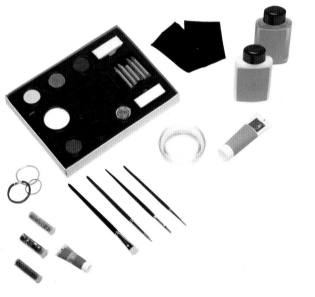

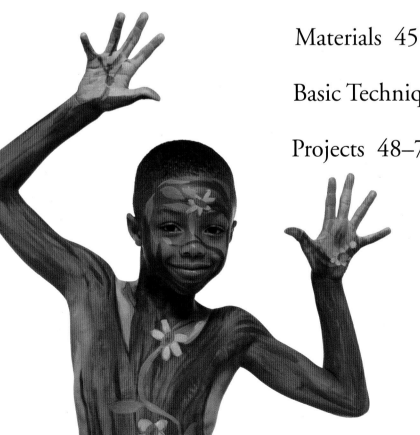

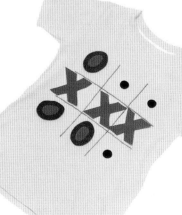

FABULOUS

FACE PAINTING & DISGUISES

Fun ideas to change the way you look!

southwater

This edition published by Southwater in 2003.

Southwater is an imprint of Anness Publishing Ltd
Hermes House, 88–89 Blackfriars Road, London SE1 8HA
tel. 020 7401 2077; fax 020 7633 9499
www.southwaterbooks.com; info@anness.com

© Anness Publishing Limited 2000, 2003

This edition distributed in the UK by
The Manning Partnership Ltd
6 The Old Dairy, Melcombe Road, Bath BA2 3LR
tel. 01225 478 444, fax 01225 478 440
sales@manning-partnership.co.uk

This edition distributed in the USA and Canada by
National Book Network
4720 Boston Way, Lanham, MD 20706
tel. 301 459 336, fax 301 459 1705 www.nbnbooks.com

This edition distributed in Australia by
Pan Macmillan Australia
Level 18, St Martins Tower, 31 Market St, Sydney, NSW 2000
tel. 1300 135 113, fax 1300 135 103
email customer.service@macmillan.com.au

This edition distributed in New Zealand by
The Five Mile Press (NZ) Ltd
PO Box 33–1071 Takapuna
Unit 11/101–111 Diana Drive Glenfield, , Auckland 10
tel. (09) 444 4144, fax (09) 444 4518
fivemilenz@clear.net.nz

The activities and projects in this book were created by:
Petra Boase – Painting Fun. T-shirt Painting and Modelling Fun
Thomasina Smith – Magical Masks, Face and Body Painting
and Modelling Fun.

Publisher: Joanna Lorenz
Editor: Lyn Coutts, Lo Somerville
Photography: John Freeman, Tim Ridley
additional Design: Caroline Grimshaw
Production Controller: Joanna King

Previously published as part of a larger Compendium:
The Really big Book of Amazing Things to Make and Do.
The Outrageously Big Activity, Play and Project Book.

Printed and bound in Hong Kong/China

3 5 7 9 10 8 6 4 2

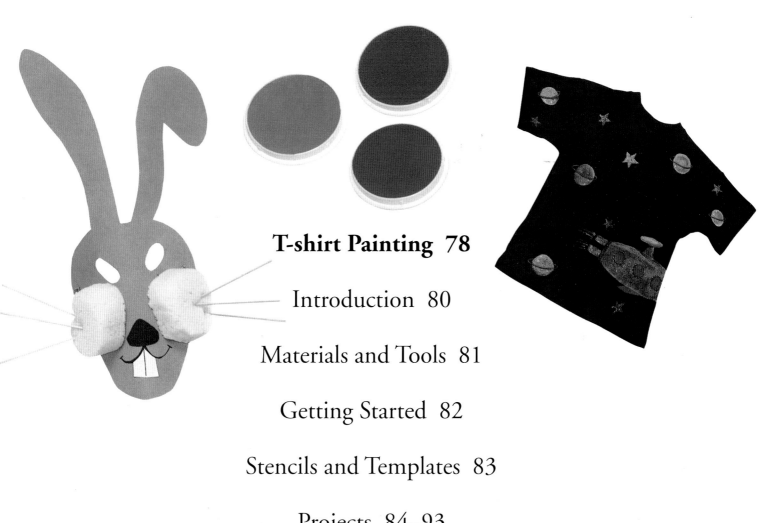

Magical
Masks

Thomasina Smith

Introduction

Masks are used to transform people and for disguise. In many ancient cultures, masks were an important part of religious and social customs. The person wearing the mask could become a god or a spirit. But masks are also important in modern culture. They are used in the re-enactment of special events, in the theater and for fun. Japanese theater relies on the actors wearing masks to portray certain characters, and some countries have street carnivals where people wear funny masks. There are even special parties, called masquerade balls, to which everyone must wear a mask.

You can make a mask to wear to a party, for dressing-up or to wear in a school play. Masks also make great wall decorations.

The Magical Masks that follow are both easy and fun to make. Cardboard, fabric and papier-mâché are good basic materials, but you can also use items such as an ice-cube tray, an old tennis ball or scouring pads. In fact, almost anything can be used in mask-making. Following are some basic techniques that will help you to make some wonderful masks.

The very scary Wicked Witch mask!

The Venetian Mask makes the wearer look very mysterious.

Fitting a mask

To make eye and mouth holes in the right positions on your mask, you need to know the distance between your eyes and the distance from your nose to your mouth. Start by tracing around a pair of glasses or swimming goggles onto your mask. Then measure the distance from the bridge of your nose to your mouth. Measure and mark this distance on your mask.

Cutting eye holes

1 Hold a paper plate in front of your face. Carefully feel where your eyes are using your fingers.

2 When you have found where your eyes are, mark the position of each one on the paper plate with a pencil.

3 Draw two circles around the marks. Make a hole in the center of the circles, then cut around the outlines.

Cutting a mouth

To cut out a mouth from a paper plate or cardboard mask, just use this simple trick.

Draw the outline of the mouth onto the back of a paper plate or cardboard. Fold the mask in half so that the center of the mouth is on the fold. Cut across the fold, following your outline. This will make sure that the cut-out mouth is even on both sides of your mask.

This mask is two masks in one. Open out the Hungry Wolf mask to reveal the Unlucky Lamb.

Attaching straps and ties

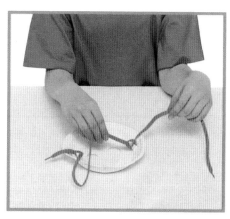

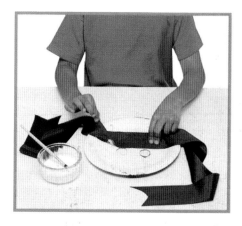

1 Cut two small holes on each side of the mask. Attach a strap to one side and place the mask on your face. Run the strap around the back of your head. Pinch the strap with your fingers when it makes contact with the second side.

2 Take the mask off, but do not let go of the strap—keep it pinched between your fingers. Put a mark on the strap where it is pinched between your fingers. Thread the strap through the second side and tie firmly at the mark.

3 Another way of attaching a strap is to glue it to the back of the mask. Mark the middle of a 1 yd long strap and position the mark in the center of the mask just below the eye holes. Allow to dry before wearing the mask.

There is something very fishy about this mask.

Safety tips

❖ Keep glues, sharp utensils and pointed objects well out of the reach of young children.

❖ Never put sharp or pointed objects near your eyes. When trying on a mask for the first time, check that there is no wet paint or glue on the back of the mask. Also check that there are no sharp edges. It is a good idea to stick clear tape around the edges of masks made with foil pie pans. Put tape around eye, nose and mouth holes as well.

❖ Plastic wrap and plastic bags should never be used to decorate a mask.

❖ Ask an adult to trim the points and remove splinters from wooden skewers or garden sticks before using.

Materials

These are the main materials and items you will need to complete the Magical Mask projects.

Basket A round cane or straw basket is best. It should be about the same size as a large plate.

Cotton You can use either cotton balls or a roll of cotton.

Corrugated cardboard This thick brown cardboard has ripples on one side and is smooth on the other. For some projects you can use corrugated cardboard recycled from boxes. Other projects require a large sheet of corrugated cardboard. It can be purchased in rolls or sheets at stationery and craft store.

Disposable kitchenware This includes things like paper plates, plastic cups and foil baking sheets or pie pans. Some of these items can be recycled from empty food packaging.

Fabric You can use a large piece of leftover plain or printed fabric or buy an inexpensive remnant at a fabric store.

Faucet nozzle This is used on the end of a kitchen faucet to direct the stream of water. You can buy plastic nozzles at hardware or kitchen stores. Use them to make noses for masks.

Funnel Small plastic funnels are available at hardware and kitchen stores. They can be used to make noses for masks.

Ice-cube tray Even an everyday item like a rectangular plastic ice-cube tray is invaluable in mask-making. As you will not be able to reuse the tray, use an unwanted tray or buy one.

Newspaper You need sheets of newspaper to cover your work surface, and strips of newspaper for making papier-mâché.

Pipe-cleaners You can find pipe-cleaners at art and craft stores. They come in various lengths and colors. To make the masks, you need an assortment of colored, striped and glittery ones.

Scouring pad This is a round pad of twisted plastic or metal thread that is used to clean pots and pans. You can buy it in lots of bright colors or in a shiny copper or silver color.

Shoelaces These are used to make ties for your masks. You can paint or buy shoelaces to match the color of your mask.

Sponge Use a felt-tip pen to mark out the shape you want on an ordinary bath or kitchen sponge, then trim with scissors.

String You will need fine plain or colored string to make ties for your masks.

Swimming goggles If you do not already have any swimming goggles, they are easy to find at sports stores. Goggles are fun to use in a mask, and make a cheap substitute for safety goggles too. Wear goggles whenever you are cutting something that may fly up into your eyes.

Tennis ball If you are making a large mask, such as the Spanish Giant, an old tennis ball cut in half and painted makes a great pair of eyes. Ask an adult to help you cut the tennis ball, as it can be quite tricky to do.

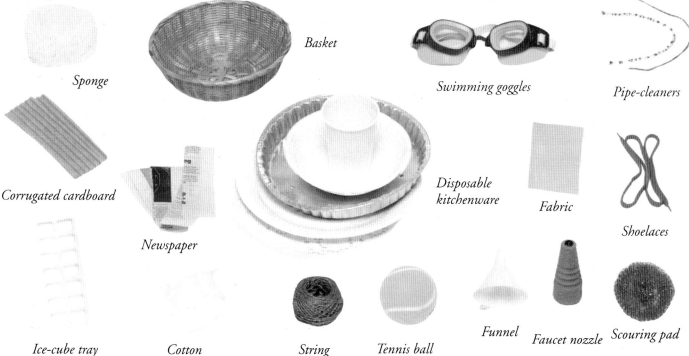

Sponge

Basket

Swimming goggles

Pipe-cleaners

Corrugated cardboard

Newspaper

Disposable kitchenware

Fabric

Shoelaces

Ice-cube tray

Cotton

String

Tennis ball

Funnel

Faucet nozzle

Scouring pad

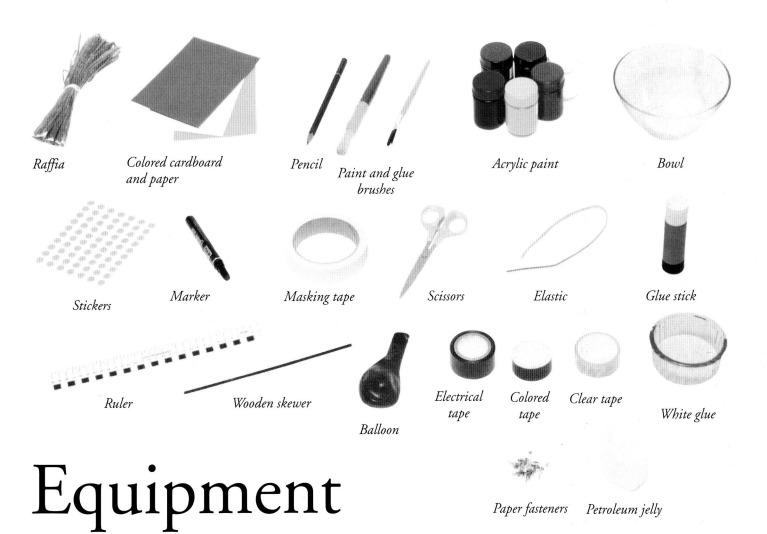

Raffia

Colored cardboard and paper

Pencil

Paint and glue brushes

Acrylic paint

Bowl

Stickers

Marker

Masking tape

Scissors

Elastic

Glue stick

Ruler

Wooden skewer

Balloon

Electrical tape

Colored tape

Clear tape

White glue

Paper fasteners

Petroleum jelly

Equipment

Acrylic paint This is a water-based paint that comes in lots of bright colors. You can also use poster paints.

Balloon You will need an ordinary round balloon to use as a mold for making a papier-mâché mask.

Colored cardboard and paper Use either scraps of leftover cardboard or paper, or buy sheets from a stationery store.

Elastic To tie a mask firmly around your head you can use a length of narrow elastic. This can be bought at fabric stores. In place of elastic, use shoelaces, string or ribbon.

Electrical tape This is also called insulating tape, and it can be bought in hardware stores. It comes in various widths and in lots of bright colors.

Glue stick This is great for sticking a piece of paper to a flat surface. Smooth out lumps before letting it dry. Always replace the lid, as glue sticks dry out quickly.

Masking tape This is useful for holding things in place while glued surfaces dry. Masking tape can be painted over.

Paper fasteners These are small, shiny metal pins with a round head and two legs. When the legs are pushed through paper or other items and opened, they fasten the items together.

Petroleum jelly This white or creamy jelly is very greasy. It is applied to a balloon before it is covered with papier-mâché. It prevents the papier-mâché from sticking to the balloon.

Raffia This flat, ribbon-like material is made from the leaves of a palm tree. It comes in tied-up bundles and in lots of bright colors. Buy it at craft or stationery stores.

Scissors If possible, you should have two pairs of scissors, one for cutting fabric and the other for cutting paper.

Stickers Use stickers in all sorts of colors, shapes and sizes as a quick way of decorating a mask.

Tapes You can use clear, colored or patterned tapes to make Magical Masks.

White glue This glue is also known as wood glue or school glue. White glue is a strong glue that can be used to bind paper, cardboard, fabric, plastic or wood surfaces.

Wooden skewers These narrow, round, pointed sticks are about 12 in long and can be bought at supermarkets. You can also use garden sticks or split canes, but ask an adult to cut them to the required length.

Basket Tiger

This mask is inspired by traditional African masks, many of which look like wild animals. Just like a real African mask, this mask is made using a natural material—a basket made from cane.
Clay and wood were also used to make masks.

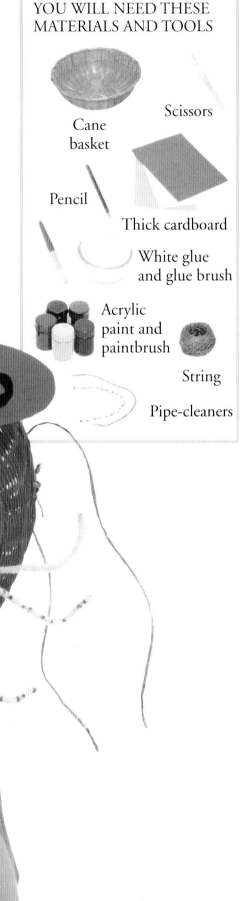

YOU WILL NEED THESE
MATERIALS AND TOOLS

Cane basket

Scissors

Pencil

Thick cardboard

White glue and glue brush

Acrylic paint and paintbrush

String

Pipe-cleaners

1 Cut a round hole in the bottom of the basket using a pair of scissors. You may need to ask an adult to help you do this. When cutting the hole, do not put your fingers under the basket.

2 Place the basket on a sheet of colored cardboard. Draw around the hole. This will become the face of the tiger. Remove the basket and draw an ear on either side of the face.

3 Cut out the face and ears. Draw and cut out a nose from a scrap of thick cardboard. Glue the nose onto the face and allow to dry. Draw, then cut out eye and mouth holes.

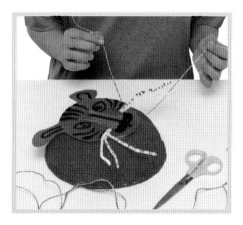

Basket animals

A cane or straw basket and cardboard can be used to make a whole zoo of animals. Follow the instructions for Basket Tiger but modify the face, ears, nose and coloring to make a monkey, a lion, an elephant or a bear. Basket masks would be perfect to use in a school play.

4 Apply glue to the back of the face and press it firmly in position over the hole in the basket. Allow to dry. Paint the basket and face orange. When dry, paint the tiger's features with black paint. Glue pipe-cleaners on each side of the nose for whiskers. Allow the glue to dry thoroughly before starting the next step.

5 Thread string through gaps in the basket, on each side of the mask. Tie the mask securely around your head.

The Basket Tiger mask is easy and quick to make. To act like a real tiger you must growl and move quietly with great stealth.

Venetian Mask

Venice is famous for its Carnival, when everyone dresses up in colorful costumes and fancy masks. This mask is not tied around your head—it is simply attached to a wooden stick. A Venetian lady would hold the mask to her face when she wanted to be mysterious, and lower it to reveal her beauty.

Handy hint

If you find that white glue is not strong enough to hold the wooden skewer securely to the mask, use tape or masking tape as well. It is also a good idea to wind tape around the bottom and the top of the skewer to keep the pipe-cleaners in place.

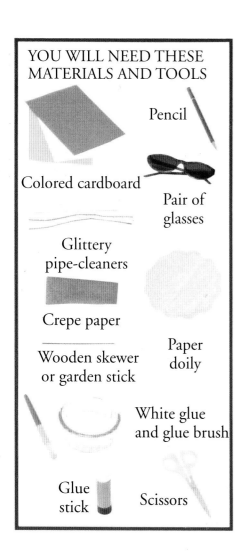

YOU WILL NEED THESE MATERIALS AND TOOLS

Pencil

Colored cardboard

Pair of glasses

Glittery pipe-cleaners

Crepe paper

Wooden skewer or garden stick

Paper doily

White glue and glue brush

Glue stick

Scissors

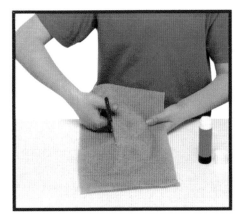

1 Place a pair of glasses on the cardboard and draw around them with a pencil. Add to your outline the fancy curves on both sides of the mask, as shown. Cut out the cardboard with scissors.

Safety!

Be careful when moving around wearing a mask. Your vision may be restricted by the size of eye holes in the mask. Take extra care when there are wooden sticks attached to the mask.

2 Apply glue to the front of the cardboard with the brush and place a piece of crepe paper on top. Smooth out the crepe paper. When the glue is dry, trim around the edges with scissors.

3 Fold the paper doily in half and cut out the semicircle in the middle. Unfold the doily and cut in half following the fold line. Pleat one half of the doily so that it looks like a fan.

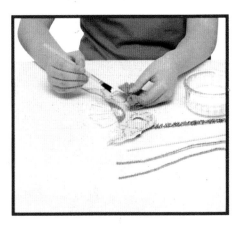

4 Glue the other half of the doily to the front of the mask with paper glue. The cut-out semicircle should be at the top of the mask. Trim around the edges so that it fits the mask perfectly. Glue the pleated doily to the top of the mask. Draw eye holes onto the front of the mask, then cut them out.

5 Ask an adult to trim any sharp ends from the wooden skewer or garden stick. Tightly wind pipe-cleaners around the skewer to cover it completely. Attach the skewer to the back of the mask with white glue and allow to dry thoroughly. Cut a rectangle of crepe paper and wind a pipe-cleaner around the middle to make a bow. Glue the bow onto the mask, as shown. Allow to dry.

You can really let your imagination run wild when decorating your Venetian Mask. The Venetians certainly do when designing their masks for the Carnival. You could add sequins and glitter, or even paint the doily gold!

Easter Rabbit

Make this fun rabbit mask to wear on Easter morning. Its plump, white cheeks are made from sponges. To make the whiskers you can use wooden skewers or plastic straws.

YOU WILL NEED THESE MATERIALS AND TOOLS

Pipe-cleaners

Cardboard

Scissors

Pencil

White glue and glue brush

Glue stick

Black marker

2 sponges

6 wooden skewers or plastic straws

Small pieces of black and white paper

Ruler

1 Draw and cut out a rabbit's face and ears, measuring 1 ft wide and 2 ft long, from thin colored cardboard. Cut out two eye holes.

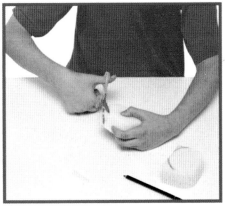

2 To make the rabbit's cheeks, draw a large circle on each sponge and cut them out. Make the circles as large as possible, then trim them to fit.

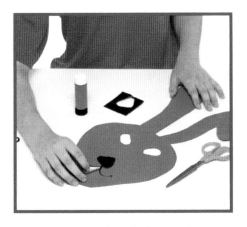

3 Draw a mouth with the marker pen. Cut out a nose from black paper and a pair of teeth from white paper. Glue them onto the mask.

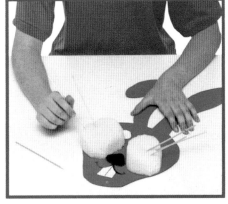

4 Glue on the sponge cheeks using white glue. The sponge will absorb the glue, so apply lots. Allow plenty of time for the glue to dry. Ask an adult to cut the pointed ends off the skewers. Dab a little white glue onto one end of each of the skewers. Insert three skewers into each sponge for the whiskers. If the whiskers are too long, ask an adult to trim them.

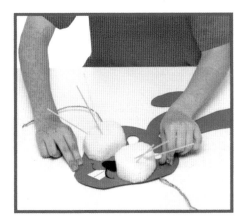

5 Make a small hole on each side of the mask. Thread a pipe-cleaner through each hole and twist the end to hold it in place. To wear the mask, hook the pipe-cleaners around your ears.

Painting your mask

If you want to paint a furry gray face onto the rabbit mask you will need— black, white and red paints, a mixing palette, water pot, and fine and medium paintbrushes. It is best if you paint the mask before gluing on the cheeks, nose and teeth.

To help you get the colors and fur just right, refer to a photograph of a rabbit in a book or magazine.

To start, mix black and white paint to make a pale gray color. Use the medium paintbrush to paint the front of the mask, but do not paint the ears. Mix a little more black into the gray to make it darker. Use this color to paint lots of short, fine lines radiating outward from the cheeks. While this dries, paint the ears pink. You can make pink by mixing white and red paint. Paint the edges of the ears gray. Paint lots of short, fine white lines, also radiating outward from the cheeks. When dry, finish making the mask.

Wicked Witch

Make yourself a wicked witch disguise
to wear to a Halloween costume party.
To complete your awful transformation,
make a broomstick from twigs and branches
and wear a black cloak over your shoulders.

Handy hint

If you cannot find a plastic funnel to
use for the witch's nose, form a cone
from a piece of cardboard.

To make a cone, cut out a circle
6 in wide. Cut the circle in half. Bend
one half so that the straight edges
overlap. Attach the edges with tape.
Trace around the base of the cone onto
the plate. Draw a slightly smaller circle
inside the outline. Cut out the small
circle. Make shorts snips up into the
base of the cone. Fold out these flaps
and push the cone into the hole. Glue
the flaps to the back of the plate.

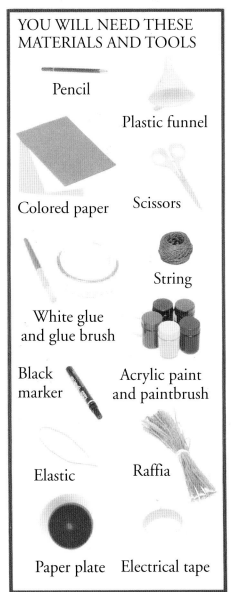

YOU WILL NEED THESE MATERIALS AND TOOLS

Pencil

Plastic funnel

Colored paper

Scissors

String

White glue
and glue brush

Black
marker

Acrylic paint
and paintbrush

Elastic

Raffia

Paper plate   Electrical tape

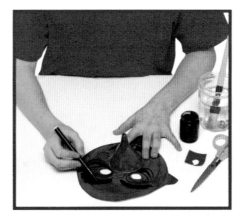

1 Draw a witch's face with a pointed chin on the back of a paper plate and cut it out. Cut out holes for eyes. Place the funnel in the center of the plate and trace around it. Cut out the circle, slightly inside the drawn line. Glue the funnel over the hole.

2 Mix a little white glue into green paint—the glue will help the paint stick to the funnel. Paint the face and funnel green. Cut out a small circle of red paper and glue it to one cheek to make a wart. Draw and color in other features with a black marker pen.

3 Undo the bundle of raffia and cut it into long lengths for the witch's hair. Tie the lengths of raffia together at one end with a piece of string. Use a piece of electrical tape to attach the bundle of raffia to the back of the plate.

4 Make a hole on each side of the mask. Thread a long length of elastic through one hole and tie it on. Put the mask on your face. Cut the elastic to the right length and knot it onto the other hole.

If this gruesome, green mask does not scare your friends and family, then nothing will. To really play the part of a witch, make up some spooky spells and carry around a pot full of plastic spiders and frogs!

Crazy Glasses

These glasses are inspired by the ones you find at joke stores. Crazy Glasses will really let you make a spectacle of yourself!

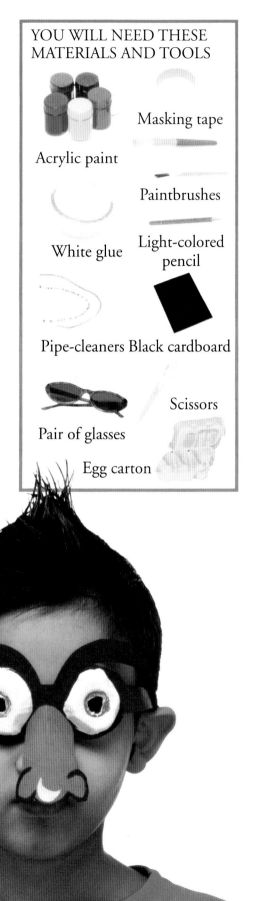

YOU WILL NEED THESE MATERIALS AND TOOLS

Acrylic paint

Masking tape

Paintbrushes

White glue

Light-colored pencil

Pipe-cleaners Black cardboard

Scissors

Pair of glasses

Egg carton

1 Draw a glasses shape on the black cardboard. Use the pair of glasses as a guide for size and for the shape around your nose. You will need to use a light-colored pencil or the outline will not show up. Cut around the outline.

2 Cut out two of the compartments from an egg carton to make the eyes. Make a hole in the center of each one for you to see through. Cut a piece of cardboard from the lid of the egg carton for the nose. Paint them and allow to dry.

3 When dry, glue the eyes and nose onto the frame of your Crazy Glasses with white glue. To make sure the nose is firmly fixed, use masking tape to hold it in position. While the glue is drying, prop up the nose with a pencil. Paint two pipe-cleaners black and allow to dry.

To finish, apply white glue to the ends of both arms of the Crazy Glasses. Wind a black pipe-cleaner several times around each glued area and allow to dry. Bend the pipe-cleaners around your ears to keep your crazy specs in place.

Fish Face

Masks can be made using almost anything! Here, a pair of swimming goggles is used to make a very fishy mask.

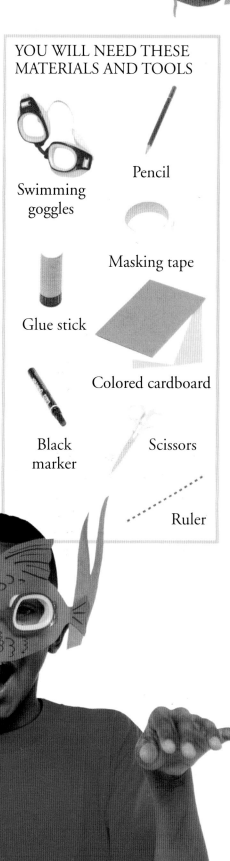

1 Draw a fish shape 10 in x 4 in on cardboard. Cut it out. Place the swimming goggles onto the fish and draw around the outline. To make this easy, hold the goggles in position with masking tape. Also, cut a small circle for the fish eye and fronds of seaweed from different colored cardboard.

2 Remove the goggles and cut out the eye holes following the lines you have drawn. Cut four small vertical slits, two on the outside edge of each eye hole. Make sure the slits are large enough to fit the strap on the goggles. Remove the strap from your goggles.

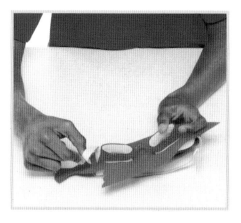

To finish, glue the eye onto the fish and use a marker pen to draw scales and fins. Glue fronds of seaweed to the mask.

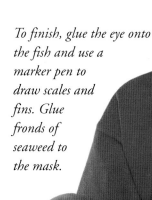

3 Push the swimming goggles into the holes of the Fish Face. If they do not fit, make the eye holes on the mask a little larger. Reattach the strap to the goggles by threading the strap through the slits in both goggles and the mask.

Hungry Wolf, Unlucky Lamb

This type of mask is called a transformation mask because it changes from one animal into another. It comes from the Pacific Northwest. This mask tells the story of an unlucky lamb eaten by a wolf.

"Watch out Lamb, the Hungry Wolf is here, and he cannot wait to gobble you up!"

1 Place an upturned plastic cup in the center of one of the pie pans. Draw around the cup with the black marker pen. Remove the cup. Inside the circle, draw a hole for your nose. Then draw eye and mouth holes. Cut out the nose, eye and mouth holes.

2 Place the cut pan inside the other pan and trace around the nose, eye and mouth holes. Separate the pans and cut around the lines. Take the pan with the outline of the circle in the center and cut it in half, straight down the middle between the eye holes.

3 Use white glue to stick the upturned plastic cup onto the back of one half of the halved pan. Position the cup on the marker line. Do not worry if the glue spreads—white glue is invisible when dry. Allow plenty of time for the glue to dry thoroughly.

5 Place the two halves of the wolf mask on top of the lamb mask—the eye and mouth holes must line up. Use masking tape to hinge the wolf masks to the lamb mask. Open the mask and make hinges on the inside. Paint over any visible tape. Tape a shoelace to the bottom of each half of the wolf mask. Tie the laces to keep the mask closed. Make a small hole through both masks on each side. Try on the mask before cutting and tying on the elastic strap.

4 To paint foil, always add a little white glue to the paint color before applying. Paint both halves of the halved pan red. Cut out red, black and white paper to make a pair of pointed ears, sharp white fangs and large oval eyes for the wolf. Paint the end of the cup black. Paint the other pan white. Use red and black paint to add the lamb's features. Paint a blue tear on the lamb's cheek. Allow the masks to dry.

To reveal the Unlucky Lamb mask, undo the shoelace tie at the front. The blue pieces of electrical tape show how the shoelaces are attached and where the hinges are placed.

Coco the Clown

If you enjoy the circus, then you will love this cheerful mask. Use colorful or shiny scouring pads to make the clown's wild hair.

Handy hint

To make Coco's hair you can use copper or silver-colored scouring pads or brightly colored plastic ones in yellow, green, purple, red or blue. Use different colored scouring pads to make Coco's hair really wild! You can buy scouring pads at supermarkets or hardware stores.

YOU WILL NEED THESE MATERIALS AND TOOLS

Pencil

2 paper plates

Scissors

White glue and glue brush

Raffia

Acrylic paints and paintbrushes

Electrical tape

6 paper fasteners

6 scouring pads

Elastic

Small plastic cap

1 Hold one of the paper plates up to your face and ask an adult to mark eye holes. Cut out the eye holes. On the back of the plate, paint your clown face. Allow the paint to dry.

2 Draw a triangular hat and bow tie on the remaining paper plate. Cut them out. Paint and decorate the hat and bow tie with paint and electrical tape. Finish the hat with a tassel of raffia. Attach the raffia with electrical tape.

3 To make the clown's nose, use the plastic cap from a tube of candy or plastic juice container. Mix a little white glue into some red paint and paint the nose. When dry, glue the nose onto the clown's face. Use white glue to stick on the hat and bow tie. Allow glue to dry.

4 Push a paper fastener through a scouring pad and position it near the top edge of the plate. Push the paper fastener through the plate and flatten the fasteners. Attach the remaining scouring pads in the same way. Make a small hole in each side of the mask. Tie the elastic to one hole, then fit the mask before tying the elastic to the other hole.

Clown outfit

To make a clown outfit very quickly, attach colorful scouring pads down the front of a T-shirt and to the front of your shoes. Electrical tape is also great for jazzing up a pair of old plain jogging pants. Use it to make stripes, checks and crazy patterns.

Bush Spirit Mask

The idea for this mask comes from the Pacific island of Papua New Guinea. It is made for ceremonies that celebrate the bush spirits, or Kovave. This cardboard and fabric mask is a simple version of the real one. The fringe at the bottom of the mask covers the wearer's shoulders and gives the effect of a bird's body.

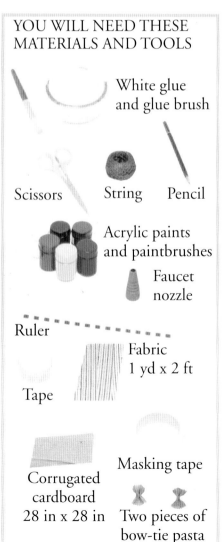

YOU WILL NEED THESE MATERIALS AND TOOLS

White glue and glue brush

Scissors   String   Pencil

Acrylic paints and paintbrushes

Faucet nozzle

Ruler

Fabric 1 yd x 2 ft

Tape

Corrugated cardboard 28 in x 28 in

Masking tape

Two pieces of bow-tie pasta

Drape the strips of fabric over your shoulders and across your face. Then you can start to strut and move like a bird.

1 Fit the piece of cardboard around your head and fix the seam with masking tape. The rippled side of the cardboard should be facing out.

4 To make the fringe, cut the fabric into ³/₄-in wide strips. Attach one end of the strips to a 28-in length of tape. Overlap the strips. Glue the fringe inside the bottom edge of the mask.

5 Make a small hole on each side near the base of the mask. Knot a piece of string to each hole and tie under the chin.

2 Glue the cardboard at the seam. Allow it to dry and remove the masking tape. Paint the nozzle brown, adding some white glue to the paint so that it sticks to the plastic. Paint brown stripes onto the cardboard. Paint between the stripes white.

3 When the paint on the nozzle is dry, attach it to the cardboard with white glue to make the bird's beak. Use plenty of glue and do not worry about spills—white glue is invisible when dry. Glue on pasta pieces for the eyes. Allow the glue to dry thoroughly.

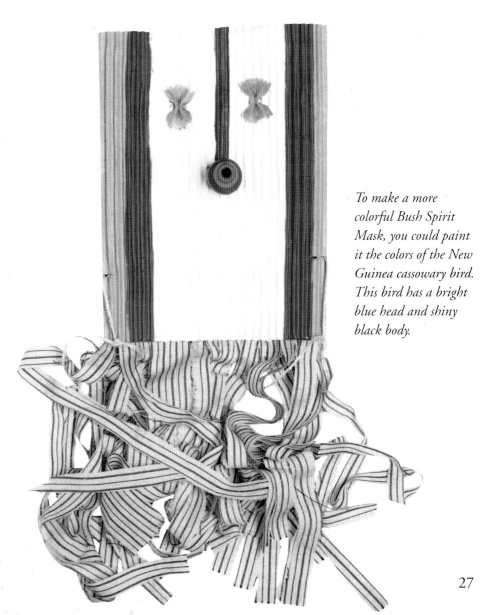

To make a more colorful Bush Spirit Mask, you could paint it the colors of the New Guinea cassowary bird. This bird has a bright blue head and shiny black body.

Beaky Bird

This mask has a beak that opens and closes. The idea comes from the ceremonial masks from the Pacific Northwest.

Papier-mâché

Papier-mâché involves gluing small squares or strips of newspaper onto a shape or mold, to make it stronger or to change its shape.

To make the glue, combine equal amounts of white glue and water in a dish. Dip the newspaper pieces into the glue and smooth them onto the shape until it is covered. Allow to dry before applying a second layer of papier-mâché.

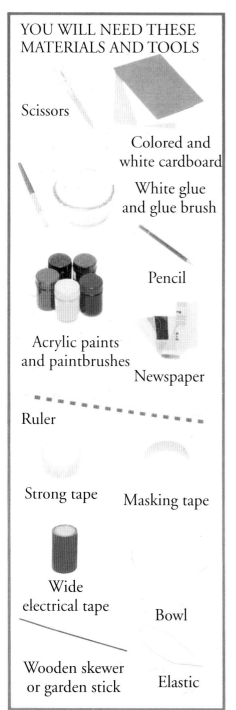

YOU WILL NEED THESE MATERIALS AND TOOLS

Scissors

Colored and white cardboard

White glue and glue brush

Pencil

Acrylic paints and paintbrushes

Newspaper

Ruler

Strong tape   Masking tape

Wide electrical tape

Bowl

Wooden skewer or garden stick   Elastic

1 Draw onto cardboard one oval shape for the face 12 in x 4 in, two triangles for the upper beak 6 in x 1¼ in and two rectangles for the lower beak 6 in x 3 in. Cut out all the pieces.

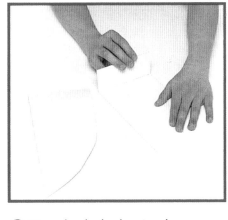

2 To make the beak, trim the two rectangles (for the lower beak) to match those shown above. Use scissors to score a fold line along the short edge of all four beak pieces. Bend each piece along the fold line to form a small flap.

3 Use masking tape to attach the curved edge of the lower beak pieces. Take one of the upper beak triangles and tape its long edges to the long edges of the lower beak. Fold the flaps inward and tape over the hole. The shape should resemble the bow of a boat. Cover the beak with papier-mâché. When dry, tape the skewer to the front of the beak. Do two more layers of papier-mâché.

4 Glue the flap of the remaining upper beak piece onto the face. When dry, paint the face and beak.

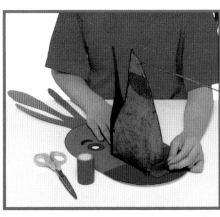

5 Cut out a plume from cardboard and glue it to the back of the mask. Hinge the bottom of the lower beak onto the mask with electrical tape.

To finish, make a small hole on each side of the mask. Tie a length of elastic to each hole. When you are ready to make Beaky Bird squawk and talk, tie the elastic at the back of your head and use the skewer to move the lower beak up and down.

Talking House

Not all masks are of animals or humans. You can also create wonderful illusions using masks of inanimate, or non-living, objects. The Talking House mask is one of these very clever illusions. Once you have made the Talking House, see how many other objects you can turn into funny masks.

Handy hint

To create a really convincing illusion, make a costume to wear with your Talking House mask. If you dress in green and tape cotton bushes onto your T-shirt, your house will become the house on the hill. To create the illusion of a beautiful garden outside your house, wear a flowery shirt. Make a path to the front door with yellow electrical tape.

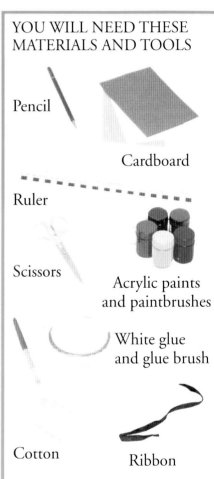

YOU WILL NEED THESE MATERIALS AND TOOLS

Pencil

Cardboard

Ruler

Scissors

Acrylic paints and paintbrushes

White glue and glue brush

Cotton

Ribbon

If you and your friends all make Talking House masks, you will have the whole street talking!

1 Draw a house (with a smoking chimney) 12 in x 10 in on a piece of cardboard. Draw in two eye holes and a hole for your nose.

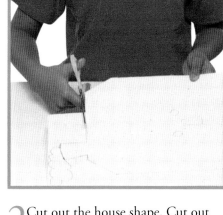

2 Cut out the house shape. Cut out the holes for the eyes and the nose.

3 Paint the house red. When dry, paint rows of bricks and roof tiles in yellow. Paint window and door frames and the trunk of a tree black.

Add as many details to your house as you like. You could even make a Talking House that is exactly like your own house!

4 Tease some cotton to resemble billowing smoke and glue it to the chimney. Lightly dab the cotton with gray paint. Repeat to make the top of the tree, but lightly dab the cotton with green paint.

5 Make two holes just above the eye holes. Thread a long piece of ribbon through the holes, as shown.

Crocodile

There is a long tradition in mask-making of using everyday materials from around the house. With this crocodile mask, an ice-cube tray takes on a new life!

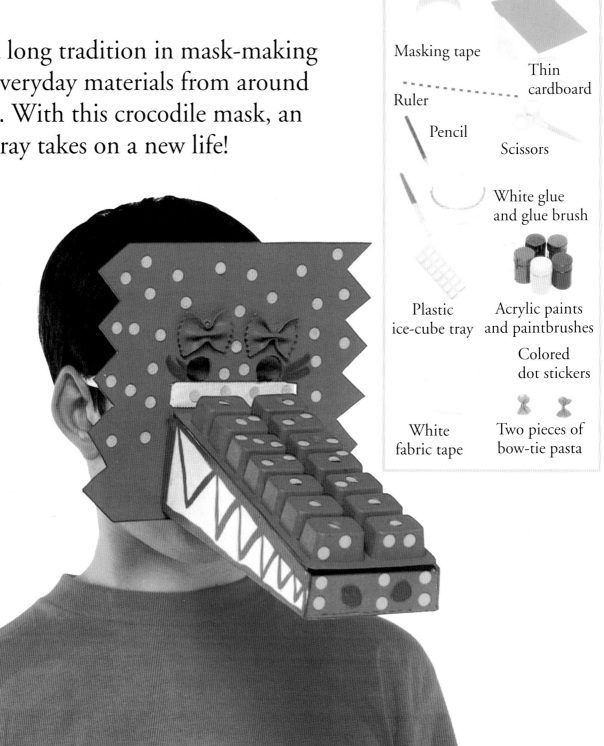

YOU WILL NEED THESE MATERIALS AND TOOLS

Masking tape

Thin cardboard

Ruler

Pencil

Scissors

White glue and glue brush

Plastic ice-cube tray

Acrylic paints and paintbrushes

Colored dot stickers

White fabric tape

Two pieces of bow-tie pasta

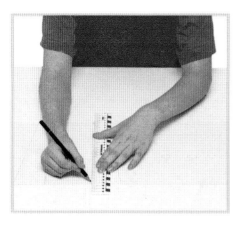

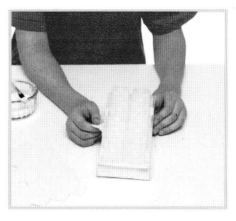

1 Draw an 8-in square on cardboard. Draw eye holes, and a zigzag line down two edges. Do two tracings of the ice-cube tray onto cardboard. Add tabs, the same depth as the tray, to every side of both tracings. Make the tabs on the long sides of one tracing, wider at one end.

2 Cut around the outlines and cut out the eyes. Make fold lines by scoring all lines on the snout with scissors. Make the lower jaw by folding and gluing the tabs together. When dry, glue the ice-cube tray on top of the snout. Use masking tape to keep things in position while the glue dries.

3 Glue the snout to the face. Carefully cut two slits in the face just above the snout, as shown. Glue pasta above the eyes. Paint the Crocodile's face and the top and front of its snout blue. Paint the sides of the snout white and mark teeth in red. When dry, cover the crocodile with colored dot stickers.

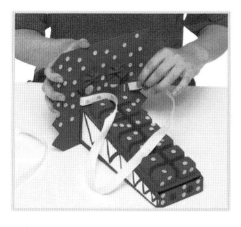

4 Thread the fabric tape through the slits, as shown. The tape will show, so decorate it with a line of dot stickers. Tie the tape around your head.

Animals with snouts

This method of creating a long snout using cardboard, can be used to make other long-snouted animals like horses, giraffes or even dogs. To adapt this snout for other less-snappy creatures, simply make the rectangles shorter and the sides wider. You can add ears and horns by simply cutting them out of cardboard and gluing them onto the face. Then all you have to do is paint and decorate your animal mask!

To make your crocodile mask look more realistic, find a photograph in a book and copy the colors. If you make two identical crocodile masks, you and a friend could play a game of snapping crocodiles.

Spanish Giant

This mask is made to sit on top of your head. Gauzy material falling from the mask covers your face. Masks like this one are used in Spanish carnivals and are often two or three times the size of a person.

Handy hint

When painting the face, make sure you leave enough space under the mouth so that the base can be trimmed. If you prefer, you could fit the mask and make holes for the elastic before you start painting.

To trim the mask, use scissors. If you find the papier-mâché too hard to cut, ask an adult to help.

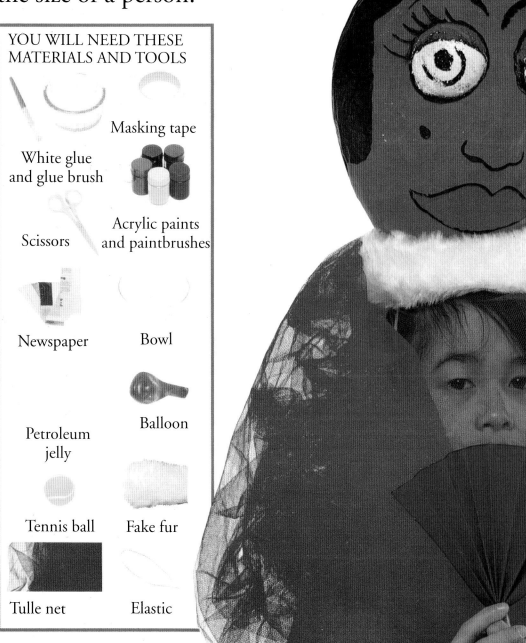

YOU WILL NEED THESE MATERIALS AND TOOLS

Masking tape

White glue and glue brush

Scissors

Acrylic paints and paintbrushes

Newspaper

Bowl

Petroleum jelly

Balloon

Tennis ball

Fake fur

Tulle net

Elastic

1 Inflate the balloon and tie a knot in the end. Cover the balloon with petroleum jelly. Make papier-mâché glue by mixing equal amounts of white glue and water. Glue strips of newspaper over the balloon to cover it. Do three layers.

2 Put the papier-mâché somewhere warm to dry. When it is hard and thoroughly dry, deflate the balloon by snipping off the end of the balloon. Pull the balloon out of the papier-mâché shell and discard the balloon.

3 Ask an adult to help you cut an old tennis ball in half. Glue the halves onto the papier-mâché shell for the eyes. Use plenty of glue and hold the halved balls in place with masking tape while the glue dries.

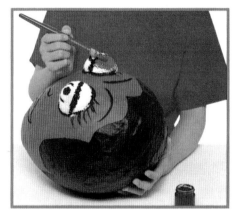

4 Paint the mask. Use a thick brush to paint large areas and a thin brush to paint details. Some areas may need two coats. Allow to dry.

5 Trim the base of the mask so that it sits on your head. Make holes near the base of the mask. Attach elastic to one hole. Get a friend to hold the mask on your head while you fit the elastic strap under your chin. Pull on the elastic to get a snug fit, then tie the elastic to the hole.

6 Tape layers of tulle net inside the base of the mask. Glue on a strip of fake fur to make a collar.

Your own design

Design your own face for the Spanish Giant. It does not have to be a woman, it could be a scary monster, a funny clown or an alien. You could even paint your own face onto the mask!

Sunshine Mask

Handy hint

Be careful when you are adding glitter to the sieve not to add too much. If you do, you will no longer be able to see through your mask!

This mask is really simple to make. You do not even need any holes for the eyes or mouth—all you have to do is decorate a sieve and a piece of paper. It could not be easier!

Use a large sieve, and make sure you draw really big sun rays. This will ensure that the mask covers your whole face.

YOU WILL NEED THESE
MATERIALS AND TOOLS

Plastic sieve

Acrylic paints and paintbrushes

White glue and glue brush

Pencil

Scissors

Yellow cardboard

Gold glitter

1 Mix white glue into some yellow paint. This should help the paint stick to the plastic. Paint the plastic part of the sieve bright yellow. Set it mesh-side down on newspaper to dry, so that little paint touches the paper.

2 Draw a circle around the sieve in the center of a large piece of yellow cardboard. Draw big sunny rays coming out from the edge of the circle. Cut out the rays and the circle from the center, as shown.

3 Discard the central paper circle. Apply some dabs of white glue to the mesh of the sieve and to the paper rays. Sprinkle gold glitter onto the glue on the rays and sieve to decorate and set in a warm place to dry.

4 Spread a line of glue around the edge of the sieve and push the rays down over the sieve. Let the mask dry completely before holding it in front of your face.

Craft tips

1. When you cut out shapes from paper, try to use up all the trimmings in other projects. For example, you could make another mask from the yellow circle that you cut out of the center of the sun.

2. Before adding glitter, fold a piece of paper in half and unfold it again. Hold the mask over the paper. As you sprinkle the glitter, the fold will make it easier to pour any left over back into the tube.

If you and your friends all make Sunshine Masks, you could look like a bunch of sunflowers!

Noh Mask

One of the most famous forms of traditional Japanese theater is called Noh. This mask is a copy from one of the characters in Noh theater. The Japanese make their masks with wood, but you can use papier-mâché.

Handy hint

In Noh performances, the mask a character wears represents a certain type of person, such as an old man or a ghost. The expression on the mask lets the audience know what the character is feeling, such as fear, joy or jealousy.

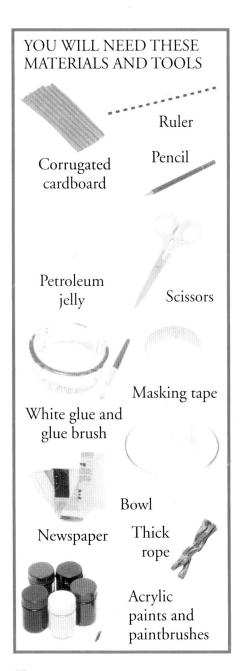

YOU WILL NEED THESE MATERIALS AND TOOLS

Corrugated cardboard

Ruler

Pencil

Scissors

Petroleum jelly

Masking tape

White glue and glue brush

Bowl

Newspaper

Thick rope

Acrylic paints and paintbrushes

Try to find out more about Japanese Noh theater. What are the plays about and what kinds of characters do they have in them? What kinds of movements do the characters make?

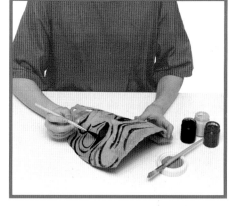

1 Cut out a face shape, measuring 12 in x 10 in, from corrugated cardboard. Draw eyes and a mouth, checking them against your face for positioning. Cut them out. Now coat the curved outside edge of a saucepan with petroleum jelly.

2 Tape the base of the mask to a saucepan. Now apply a layer of papier-mâché to the mask. Let dry and then repeat. Once dry, remove the mask from the mold and add a third layer of papier-mâché. Fold the newspaper strips around the eye and mouth holes to make smooth edges.

3 Combine red and yellow acrylic paint to make an earthy orange color. Paint the mask. Set it in a warm place to dry before painting on black lines for the facial features.

4 Make a beard by piercing three holes in the chin of the mask. Fray the rope and tie two strands through each hole. For the strap, make a hole on each side of the mask. Tie a length of rope through each hole and attach at the back of your head.

Craft tips

Before you paint the facial features on your mask, practice painting long, curved lines on a sheet of scrap paper. If you make more than one Noh mask, you could experiment with different facial expressions.

If you and a friend both make masks, you could put on a play. A traditional Noh performance usually lasts about eight hours—but yours can be shorter, of course!

Glowing Skeleton

This spooky skeleton glows in the dark and is the perfect costume to make for Halloween. It glows because it is painted with luminous paint.

Handy hint

You do not have to use white luminous paint to color your skeleton mask. It would look just as effective if you made it sickly yellow, ghoulish green or even really scary pink!

You could decorate an old black T-shirt to complete the skeleton look. Pin or sew on strips of cotton cut from an old sheet.

YOU WILL NEED THESE MATERIALS AND TOOLS

Light-colored pencil

Scissors

2 large pieces of black and white cardboard

Small can of luminous paint

Paintbrush

White glue and glue brush

Elastic

1 Draw a skeleton face on the black cardboard using a light-colored pencil. Place the white cardboard under the black cardboard and hold the two pieces firmly together. Cut out the face, including holes for the eyes, cutting through both layers of cardboard.

2 Trim the white skeleton all around the edge to make it slightly smaller than the black skeleton. Enlarge the eye sockets by about ½ in. Cut out a nose and a mouth. Then cut the mouth off to make the jaw bone.

3 Paint the white cardboard all over with luminous paint. Make sure you read the instructions on the can carefully, and use it in a well-ventilated room. Now allow the mask to dry in a warm place.

4 Glue the white skeleton face onto the black cardboard. Let dry. Make a hole on each side for the elastic strap and tie the ends. Now close the curtains and turn off the lights!

Craft tips

To prevent the black and white cardboards from slipping as you cut out shape, you could hold them down with paper clips or masking tape. Also, if you can't use luminous paint, you can use white ready-mixed paint mixed with white glue instead.

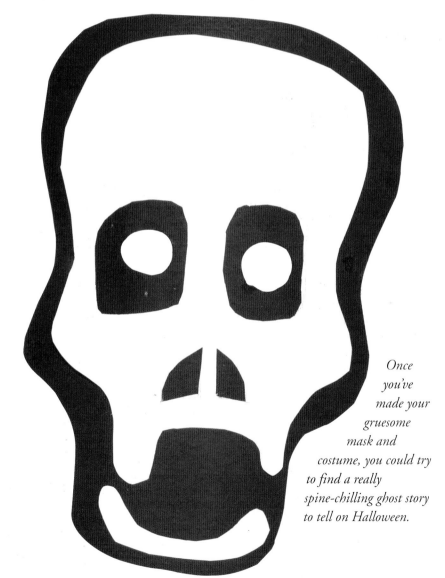

Once you've made your gruesome mask and costume, you could try to find a really spine-chilling ghost story to tell on Halloween.

Face and Body Painting

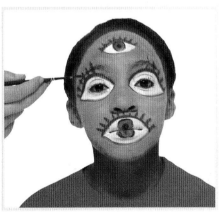

Thomasina Smith

Introduction

When your friends see your Spotted Puppy face painting, they will all want it done!

Face and body painting is a tradition that goes back thousands of years. In many ancient cultures, face and body painting was used to camouflage tribespeople when they went hunting. In other societies, face and body painting was an important part of religious ceremonies and cultural customs.

In our society today, we use face and body painting mostly to have fun and to entertain. You can face paint yourself for special occasions, costume parties, school plays or to go to a wonderful street carnival. Even putting on ordinary make-up is a form of face painting.

Become anyone you want

Face painting can transform you into someone, or even something, entirely different. With little more than a collection of face paint colors, sponges and brushes you can become a Prowling Leopard, a Spotted Puppy, a Disco Diva or even a many-eyed alien.

Body painting

There is no reason for the face painting fun to stop at your neck. You can also paint your body and limbs using exactly the same materials. Watch your hands being transformed into a proud Stag, a very rare species of Octopus, a Little Devil and even a Digital Soccer Star. Once you realize the possibilities and how easy it is to create some very funny characters, there will be no stopping you!

The only difference between face and body painting is that body painting can take longer. So, be patient and try not to laugh when a ticklish spot is being painted.

You can paint just one hand or your whole body. This funny character is the very rare pentapus. It is an octopus with only five tentacles.

Someone to help

It is very difficult to do your own face and body painting. The best idea is to ask a patient friend or adult to help. You can always promise your make-up artist that you will paint their face or body in return.

Before you get out the face paints and brushes, read through the information on Basic Techniques on the following pages. This information will show you how to achieve stunning effects and a professional finish.

To give Super Robot's face a metal-like finish, it has been painted with silver face paint.

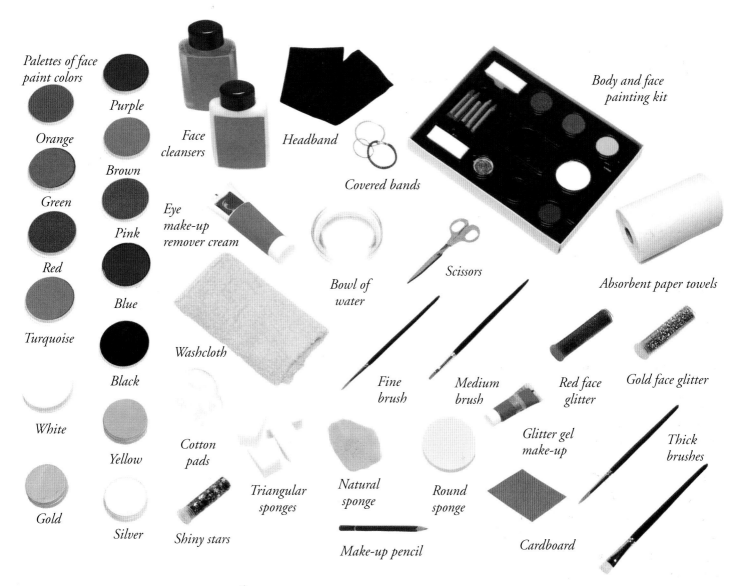

Palettes of face paint colors

Purple

Orange

Brown

Green

Pink

Red

Blue

Turquoise

Black

White

Yellow

Gold

Silver

Face cleansers

Headband

Covered bands

Body and face painting kit

Eye make-up remover cream

Bowl of water

Scissors

Absorbent paper towels

Washcloth

Fine brush

Medium brush

Red face glitter

Gold face glitter

Cotton pads

Triangular sponges

Natural sponge

Round sponge

Glitter gel make-up

Thick brushes

Shiny stars

Make-up pencil

Cardboard

Materials

Brushes You can buy special make-up brushes, or you can use good-quality watercolor brushes. You will need three brushes to complete the projects in this book—a fine, a medium and a thick brush.

Face glitter This is specially made to be used on the face. It is available at specialty stores.

Face paints These are available in kits or in individual palettes. Buy professional face paints because they are easy to use, give a very good finish and are long-lasting.

Glitter gel make-up This is a clear, gel make-up that contains colored glitter.

Make-up remover creams and cleansers These lotions will remove face paint without stinging. Always ask an adult before using any type of make-up removing product.

Natural sponge You can buy an inexpensive natural sponge at drugstores and some supermarkets. The texture of this sponge makes it ideal for creating a dappled effect.

Round sponge This smooth, round sponge is used for applying a base coat of face paint.

Shiny stars These tiny stars are made specially to be used on the face. They come in tubes and can be bought at specialty stores. Stars can be glued to the face with special face glue.

Triangular sponges These are standard make-up sponges. It is a good idea to have two or three so that you do not have to wash them every time you change face paint colors.

Washcloth and absorbent paper towels Use these for wiping excess paints off your face.

Basic Techniques

Before you start, protect clothing with an old shirt or towel. It is a good idea if the make-up artist protects his or her clothing too. Cover the work surface with absorbent paper towels and lay out your materials. Always have a bowl of water handy.

Dip the brushes and sponges into water to dampen them before loading them with face paint. Always wash brushes when changing colors. When the water becomes discolored, replace it with clean water.

How to apply the base color

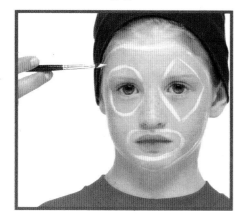

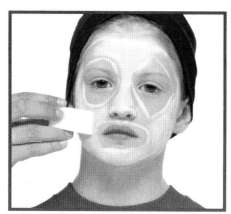

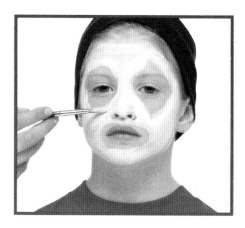

1 Use a medium or thick brush to paint the outline of a circle around the face and any other features. Paint the outlines in the base color. The instructions will always state which color should be used.

2 Dampen a round or triangular sponge in water. Rub the sponge gently around the face paint palette a few times to load sufficient color onto the sponge. Fill in the outline with base color.

3 When the outline is filled in, use a brush to neaten the edges. Use the sponge to get an even finish. In some cases, a second base coat will need to be applied to achieve this. Allow the face paint to dry between coats.

How to apply a two-color base

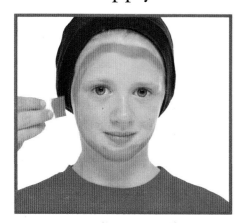

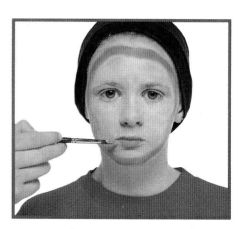

1 Outline the face using a triangular sponge or a round sponge folded in half. The instructions will always state which color to use.

2 Use a clean sponge to apply the second color. This color will go inside the outline. To make the colors merge, go over with a damp sponge.

3 When the outline is filled in, use a fine or medium brush to neaten the edges. Use the brush to touch up gaps around the nose, eyes and mouth.

Body painting

The technique for applying a base color or second color to the body or limbs is the same as for face painting.

Before starting body painting, put on the clothes you want to wear. Pulling clothes over the body painting may smudge it. Protect these clothes with an old shirt or towel. Always cover the work surface or floor with lots of absorbent paper towels or dishcloths.

Remember when wearing body paint that it will rub off onto furniture, clothes and anything you handle.

Removing make-up

Face and body paints can be easily washed off with mild soap and water. There is no need to rub hard.

Glitter gel make-up, face glitter, shiny stars and make-up glue are best removed using make-up remover creams and cleansers applied to cotton. Use special eye make-up remover cream to clean the sensitive skin around the eyes.

Always check with an adult before using any type of make-up remover, cleanser or cream.

Safety tips

It is a good idea to buy proper face paints. They will be more expensive than some alternatives, but they are easier to apply and therefore gentler on the skin. Some face paints are specially made for sensitive skins.

When you have finished face painting, gently rinse the surface of the palette under water. Wipe around the edge of the palette with a paper towel to remove excess face paint before replacing the lid.

If you do these things your face paints will remain clean, moist and ready to use.

Lay out a cloth. Apply the paint with a dampened sponge.

Allow the base to dry before applying the second color.

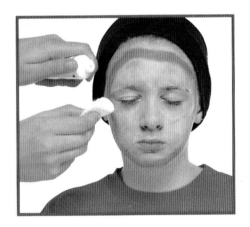

Close your eyes when face paint is being removed from around the eyes.

Dry your face and remove any traces of face paint with an old towel.

You must never use craft paints, felt-tip pens, crayons, craft glues or other stationery items on your face. They may cause an irritation.

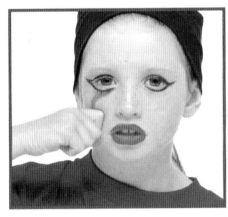

Try not to accidentally touch wet face paint, as it will cause the paint to smudge. Even when dry, face paint will smudge if it is rubbed.

Sea World

Would you like to be transformed into a living marine fantasy? It is easy and lots of fun. The crab painted around your mouth will twitch every time you smile or talk. When you blink your eye, the fish will look as though it is moving.

Handy hint

It is a good idea to wear an old towel around your neck and shoulders while your face is being painted. The towel will protect your clothes. It also provides your make-up artist with a handy place to wipe paint smudges from his or her hands and fingers.

Do not use a good towel—some dark face paints may leave a faint mark.

YOU WILL NEED THESE MATERIALS

Absorbent paper towels

Bowl of water

Face paints (brown, turquoise, orange, yellow, blue, pink, red, green, black)

Triangular sponge

Headband or covered bands

Fine and thick brushes

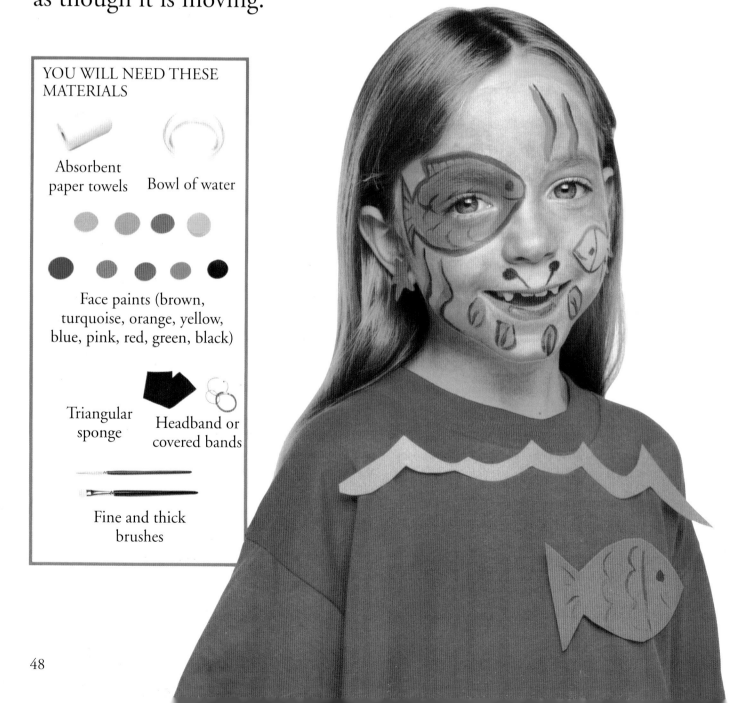

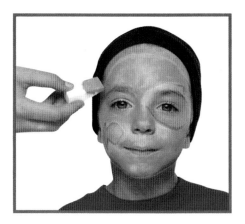

1 Tie the hair back. Paint a brown outline of a fish around one eye and on one cheek. Do this with the fine brush. Paint a turquoise circle around the face. Fill the circle using the sponge.

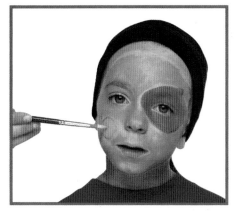

2 When the turquoise face paint is thoroughly dry, use the thick brush to paint one fish a glowing orange color and the other a bright yellow. Allow to dry.

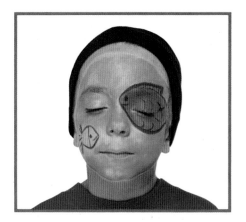

3 Paint the eyes, mouth, scales and fins onto the fish, using blue face paint and a fine brush. You must sit as still as possible while this is being done, as it is tricky work!

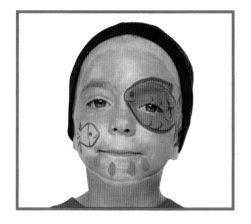

4 Break into a smile while your lips are being painted pink. Paint four pink crab claws just below the lower lip. The fine brush works best for detail work like this.

5 Use blue paint and a clean fine brush to outline and decorate the claws. Paint the face of the crab on the lower lip and draw in the stalks. Paint the crab's eyes red.

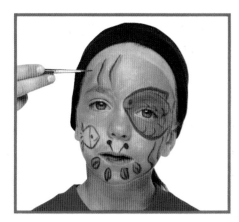

6 Use the fine brush to paint wavy green fronds of seaweed onto the forehead. To make the seaweed stand out, outline it in black face paint.

Underwater outfit to match

There is no need to spend money or lots of time making an outfit to go with your face painting. All you really need are a sea-blue T-shirt and leggings, sheets of cardboard, felt-tip pens, scissors, double-sided tape and your imagination!

Draw some fishy, underwater-type creatures or vegetation onto cardboard with the felt-tips pens. These drawings can be as large or as small as you like as long as they will fit on your T-shirt. Cut out the shapes. Press a piece of double-sided tape to the back of each shape. Peel off the protective backing and press the shape onto your T-shirt.

Here are some ideas to get you started—tropical fish with trailing fins, a pod of dolphins, corals, shells and seaweeds. You could even include a pirate's treasure chest. When your Sea World fantasy is over, simply peel the pieces of cardboard off your T-shirt.

Super Robot

This robot has supernatural abilities. Its radar vision can detect when enemy craft are approaching. The reflective metal helmet protects the robot during intergalactic battles. To make the helmet, cover a large, empty cereal box with aluminum foil.

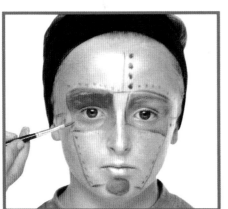

1 Tie the hair back. Close your eyes and mouth while your face is painted with the silver face paint using the round sponge. To make the silver stand out, apply two coats. Allow to dry.

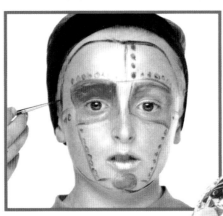

2 Use the fine brush to paint purple lines onto the face, as shown. Paint small purple dots beside the lines using the tip of the fine brush. This is the robot's reflective metal casing.

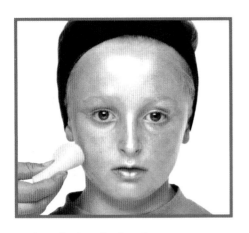

3 Paint the circle below the mouth with blue face paint using the medium brush. Then fill in the outlines around the eyes with blue face paint.

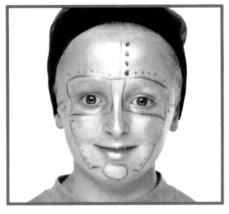

4 Wash the fine brush. Use the fine brush to paint a black outline around the face and to add more detail.

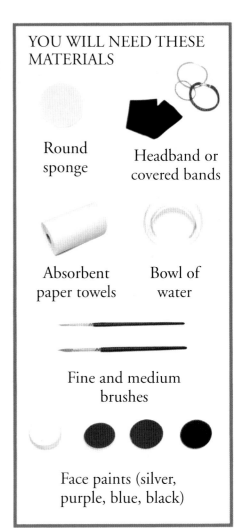

Pirate of the High Seas

Welcome aboard, landlubbers! Meet one of the nastiest villains that ever sailed the high seas.

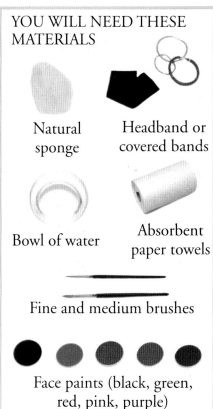
A costume for the pirate is easy to put together. All you need is a plain or striped T-shirt, a pair of baggy trousers, a sword, a rope and a head scarf.

1 Tie the hair back. Use black face paint and the fine brush to paint the moustache. It is a good idea to start at the center of the lip and work outward. Stay still while this is being done.

2 Paint the outline for the eye patch with the fine brush. Close your eye while the outline is filled with black. Paint a bushy eyebrow. Then paint the green straps for the eye patch.

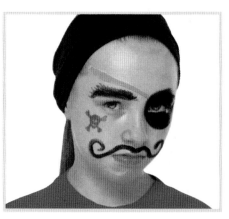

3 Paint the skull and crossbones tattoo with red face paint and the fine brush. Use the medium brush to paint the pointy, black goatee.

4 Use the natural sponge to dab the nose with pink face paint. Then dab purple face paint over the top of the pink.

Halloween Witch

Witches are an essential part of the Halloween tradition. This witch is a horrible shade of green—perhaps she ate someone nasty! She has a wrinkled face and lots of hairy warts. No wonder she does not look happy. To feel right at home in the role of a witch, why not make a broomstick from long twigs and have a spider for a pet?

Halloween Witch is wearing a black T-shirt draped with strands of purple raffia. Spiders and other creepy things cling to her clothes and hair.

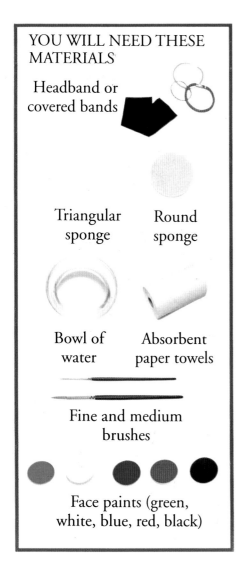

YOU WILL NEED THESE MATERIALS

Headband or covered bands

Triangular sponge

Round sponge

Bowl of water

Absorbent paper towels

Fine and medium brushes

Face paints (green, white, blue, red, black)

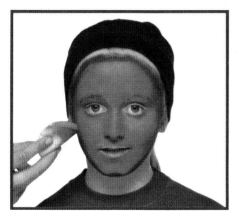

1 Tie the hair back. Use the triangular sponge to make a purple outline around the face. Fill the outline with green face paint using the round sponge. Blend the colors with the round sponge.

2 Before the green face paint dries, use the medium brush to paint above and below the eyes with white face paint. Dab this on quickly with the round sponge so that it will mix with the base color.

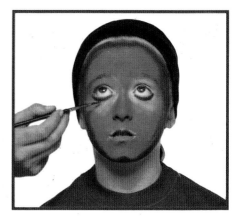

3 Mix white and blue face paints to make light blue. Paint the lower lip light blue using the medium brush. Look up toward the ceiling and keep your head still while a red line is painted under both eyes.

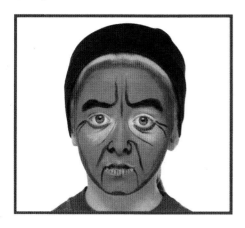

4 Paint black bushy eyebrows and wrinkles. Paint creases on the lips. Witches rarely smile, which is why they have deep frown lines.

5 Use the tip of the fine brush to paint red circles on the chin and forehead. Clean the fine brush before outlining the circles in black. Keep using the fine brush to paint black hairs sprouting from the warts.

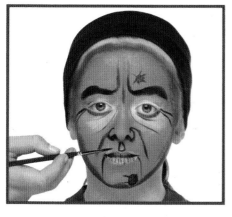

6 Use the fine brush and black face paint to accentuate the lines under the nose and add other gruesome features.

Bind together lots of twigs and branches to make a broom. Halloween Witch needs a broomstick for getting about and for sweeping up around the cauldron.

Spotted Puppy

There is only one thing more adorable than a puppy...a spotted puppy. The face painting for this extra-cute canine is easy to do. It is perfect for someone trying their hand at face painting for the very first time.

If Spotted Puppy is going to a costume party, she had better behave. No jumping on the furniture or chewing everything in sight.

YOU WILL NEED THESE MATERIALS

Headband or covered bands

Natural sponge

Round sponge

Bowl of water

Absorbent paper towels

Fine and thick brushes

Face paints (pink, white, black)

1 Tie hair off the face. Use a thick brush to paint a thick pink circle around the edge of the face. Close your eyes and mouth while your face is being painted white with the round sponge. Do two coats if necessary.

2 Use the fine brush to paint a black circle around one eye and around the nose. Paint a black line from the base of the nose to the upper lip. Paint two black lines from the corners of the mouth to the jawline.

3 Color the nose pink using the thick brush. Paint black dots on the nose with the fine brush. Dab pink face paint on either side of the mouth with a natural sponge. The sponge will create a dappled effect.

4 Make a smile while your lips are being painted. Use the fine brush to paint the upper lip black. Then paint the lower lip red.

5 Use the fine brush to paint black dots onto the cheeks. Paint circles onto the forehead, cheeks and chin with the fine brush. Paint the circles black. Close your eyes while a line is painted onto both eyelids.

To make the outfit, cut out circles of paper and stick them to a T-shirt and headband with double-sided tape. Instead of painting your hands, you could wear socks covered with paper spots on your hands.

6 Paint the back of the hands white using the round sponge. Paint black lines on the fingers and four circles.

Octopus

This is a very rare and unusual species of octopus because it has only five tentacles instead of eight. Perhaps it should be called a pentapus—"penta" meaning five. If you let the pentapus get wet, he will disappear!

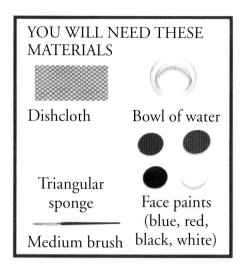

YOU WILL NEED THESE MATERIALS

Dishcloth

Bowl of water

Triangular sponge

Face paints (blue, red, black, white)

Medium brush

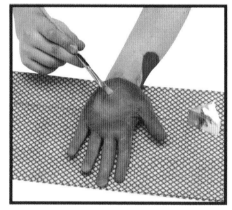

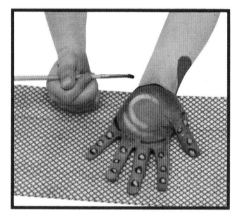

1 Lay a dishcloth on your work surface. Apply blue face paint to your hand with the triangular sponge. Allow to dry for a few minutes, then apply another coat with the medium brush. Allow to dry.

2 Turn your hand over and paint the palm pink. To make a strong pink color, mix red and white face paints. Apply the pink using the sponge. Apply a second coat with the medium brush. Allow to dry.

3 With the medium brush, paint white dots on your fingers. Allow to dry for a few minutes. Outline the white dots (suckers) with a fine line of black face paint.

Make a mini-stage for Octopus to perform on by decorating an empty cardboard box with paint and paper. You will need to leave the top of the box open so that you can put your hand onto the stage. Cut the front of the box to resemble draped stage curtains.

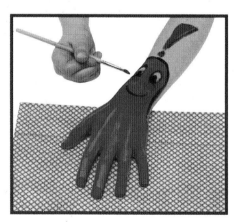

4 When the paint is dry, turn over your hand and paint the face of the octopus onto the blue background. Paint red lines down the fingers and an exclamation mark (!) above the head.

Stag

This painted hand puppet captures the elegant beauty of a proud stag. The antlers are formed using the little finger and first finger. Pinch together the two middle fingers and thumb to make the head.

YOU WILL NEED THESE MATERIALS

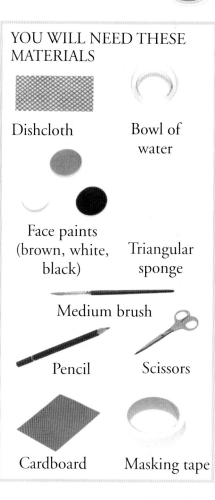

Dishcloth   Bowl of water

Face paints (brown, white, black)   Triangular sponge

Medium brush

Pencil   Scissors

Cardboard   Masking tape

1 Rest your hand on a dishcloth. Apply brown face paint with the sponge. Allow to dry. Use the brush to apply streaks of light brown face paint. Paint the ends of your thumb and two middle fingers black.

2 Pinch your fingers together to make the stag's head and antlers. Paint the eye white, as shown. Outline the eye with black and paint eyelashes.

To finish, draw two antlers onto cardboard. At the base of each antler draw a narrow strip 2 in long. Cut the antlers out. Wrap the strips around your fingers and tape the ends.

3 Cut out a ¾-in circle of blue cardboard to complete the eye. Paint a black dot in the middle. Tape the eye onto your middle finger, as shown. Paint over the tape.

Flowering Tree

This body painting of a tree is so realistic you could almost hide undetected in a tropical jungle. Even the flowers winding their way up the trunk are exotic looking. If you moved your arms as though they were branches swaying in the wind, your camouflage would be complete.

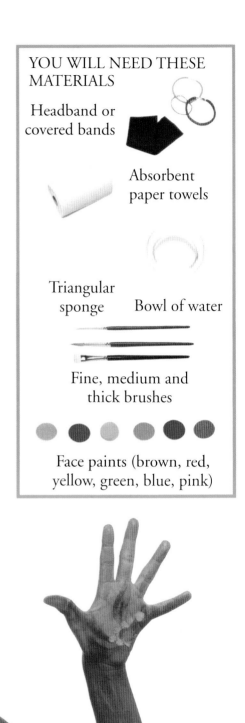

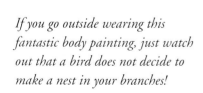

If you go outside wearing this fantastic body painting, just watch out that a bird does not decide to make a nest in your branches!

58

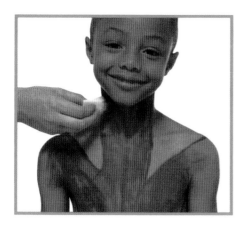

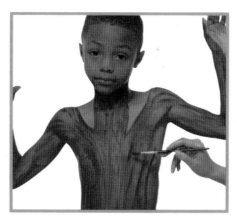

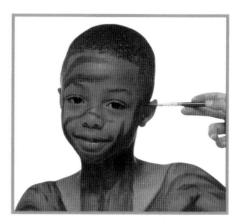

1 Tie the hair back. Use the medium brush to paint the brown outline of the tree trunk onto the chest and back. Use the sponge to fill in with brown face paint. Make shades of brown by adding red or yellow to brown.

2 Paint the front and the back of the arms (the branches) in the same way. Extend the paint onto the hands but taper it to resemble the end of a branch. Add the texture of the bark using dark brown face paint.

3 Use the thick brush and brown face paint to paint branches up the neck and onto the face. Make the branches twist and turn. Allow the paint to dry thoroughly before starting the next step.

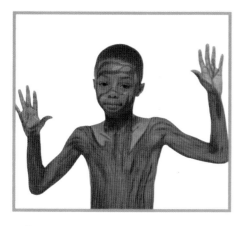

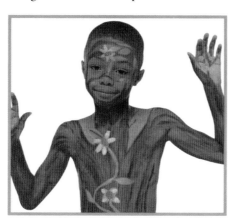

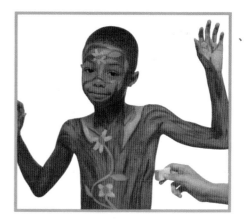

4 Wash the brush and sponge. Squeeze the sponge to get rid of excess water. Draw outlines for the leaves in green face paint. Fill in the outlines using the thick brush.

5 Paint a green stem spiraling up the trunk and linking all the leaves. Paint the flowers blue using a thick brush. Do two coats. When dry, paint the centers pink.

6 Use the clean sponge to paint in the background sky. This means filling in the unpainted areas with blue face paint. Apply it unevenly to look like a cloudy sky.

Making face paints go further

When you are painting a large area, like a person's body, with face paints, always apply the paints with a triangular, round or natural sponge. Before dipping the sponge into the paint, dampen it in a little water. This will make the face paint go on easier and also make it go further. To even out face paint, dampen the sponge and wipe it gently over the area where the color is concentrated.

You can mix face paint colors just as you would ordinary acrylic or poster paints. If you need only a little amount of a mixed color, do the mixing on the lid of the palette. For large amounts of a mixed color, use a smooth plate. To add sparkle to your face paint colors, mix in glitter gel make-up, face glitter or sequins.

Disco Diva

To dazzle all the other dancers at the disco, add a sparkle or two to your face with glitter gel make-up. It comes in lots of colors, so choose your favorites. Glitter gel make-up is easy to use, but it can be a little messy.

A diva is someone who is excellent at doing something. A Disco Diva is someone who knows all the dance moves and how to make them.

60

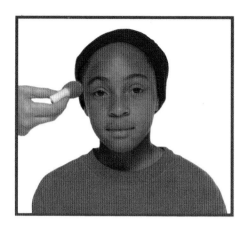

1 Tie the hair back. Apply a wide circle of pink face paint around the edge of the face using a damp round sponge. Do not worry if the circle is not perfect—the edges can be neatened with the fine brush.

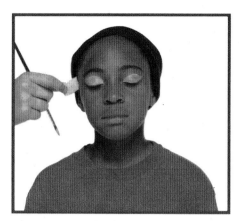

2 Paint a turquoise line with the fine brush from the inside corner of each eye up to the end of each eyebrow. Fill in with turquoise using the thick brush. Blend in the color with a damp natural sponge.

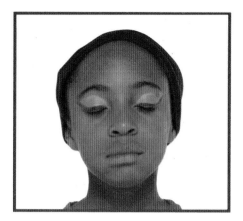

3 When the face paint is dry, paint two thin black lines onto the eyelids, as shown. Start the line from the inside corner of each eye and move outward. Keep your eyes closed until the paint has dried.

Sparkling extras

This would be a great time to spray your hair with a glitter hair spray. To remove the sparkling dust, rinse or brush your hair. You can buy glitter hair spray at specialty theatrical stores and some drugstores.

4 Use the glitter gel brush to paint the gold glitter gel onto the forehead, nose, eyelids and around the mouth. Glitter gel make-up is quite runny so apply it sparingly and carefully. When dry, apply another coat if necessary.

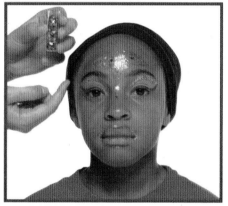

5 While the glitter gel is wet, gently press some stars onto the forehead and nose. Do not put lots of stars in one place—they will fall off. If the gel dries before the stars are in place, apply some more gel.

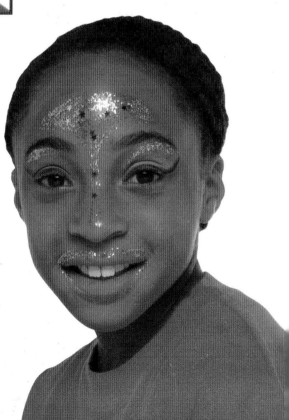

6 Stretch your lips into a broad smile while bright pink face paint is applied to your lips with the thick brush. You have every reason to smile, Disco Diva, because you are ready to go dancing!

Prowling Leopard

Face painting is a great way to be transformed into an animal, especially an exotic jungle creature like this sleek, spotted leopard. To make your face look lean, mean and hungry, the outline around the face is a special shape.

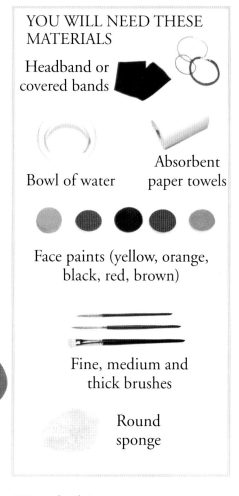

YOU WILL NEED THESE MATERIALS

Headband or covered bands

Bowl of water

Absorbent paper towels

Face paints (yellow, orange, black, red, brown)

Fine, medium and thick brushes

Round sponge

Handy hint

If you use face paint on your hands, do not forget to keep your hands away from water. Even small splashes of water will wash away face paint.

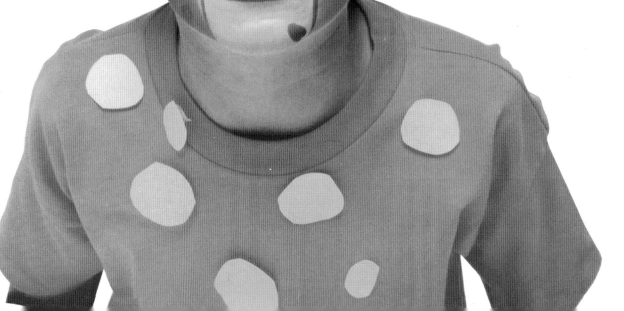

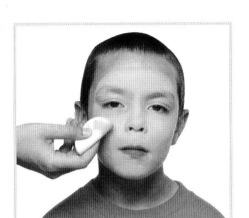

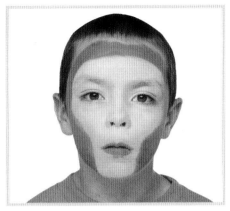

1 Tie the hair back. Paint a yellow circle around the face with a medium brush. Fill in the circle with yellow face paint applied with a round sponge. Try to apply the face paint smoothly and evenly.

2 Use the thick brush to paint an outline around the face in orange face paint. Shape the outline, as shown. Neaten the edges with the fine or medium brush. Allow the base color to dry thoroughly before continuing.

3 Close your eyes while black lines are painted on your eyelids. A fine brush will be needed for this. Paint the nose and the upper lip with black face paint. Paint the line that runs from the upper lip to the nose.

4 Even leopards can raise a smile so that their lower lip can be painted bright red. A fine brush will be needed to paint the lips.

5 Use the fine brush to paint the sweeping eyebrows, spots and lines on the face brown. Try to do this as neatly as possible.

6 Paint tiny brown dots below the nose with the fine brush. Paint lines from these dots to make the leopard's whiskers. Growl!

Look out, leopard about!

To make yourself a really convincing leopard takes a little more than just face paint. You will have to prowl like a leopard—silently—and growl like a leopard. It also helps if you dress like this sleek lord of the jungle.

To make the ears, cut two oval shapes from orange cardboard. Fold along the bottom to form a flap. Draw a line in felt-tip pen on each ear, as shown. Apply special make-up glue to the base of the flaps and press them onto your forehead. Adding spots to an orange T-shirt (and even jogging pants or leggings) is easy. Simply cut yellow circles from cardboard and use double-sided tape to attach them to the front and back of the T-shirt.

You can either paint the paws using face paint or wear a pair of gloves or socks on your hands. You can decorate the gloves or socks with circles and strips of cardboard. Attach the cardboard with double-sided tape.

Fake Tattoo

A tattoo is simple to do when it is done with face paint. Better still, it will wash off with soap and water. Tattoos can be painted anywhere on your body. This tattoo consists of a banner, a heart and someone's initials.

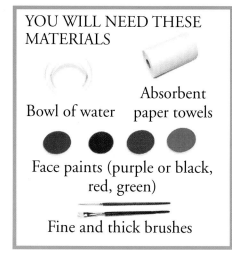
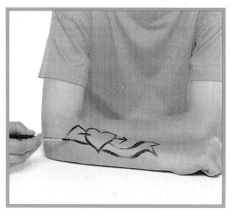

1 Paint the outline of the tattoo in purple or black using the fine brush.

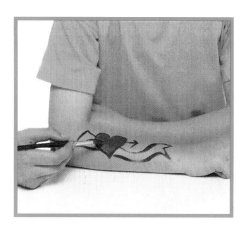

2 Allow the outline to dry before painting the heart red. Do this with the thick brush.

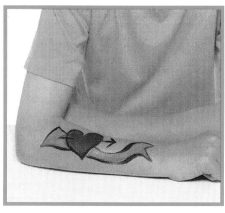

3 Clean the thick brush before using it to paint the banner green. Do two coats, if necessary.

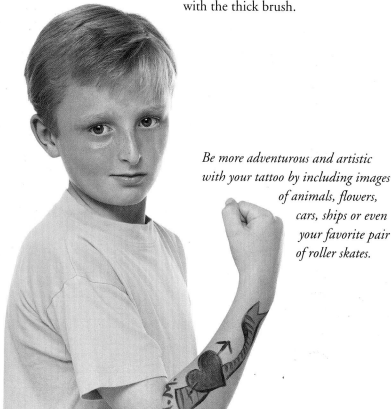

Be more adventurous and artistic with your tattoo by including images of animals, flowers, cars, ships or even your favorite pair of roller skates.

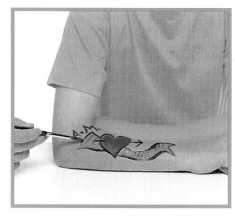

4 Paint the initials in purple or black face paint using the fine brush. Clean the fine brush. Decorate the banner with thin red stripes using the fine brush.

Jewels Galore

Use face paints to create fantastic jewelry. Do it for fun or to jazz up a costume. Imagine how amazed your friends will be when you turn up at a party dripping with diamonds, rubies and sapphires!

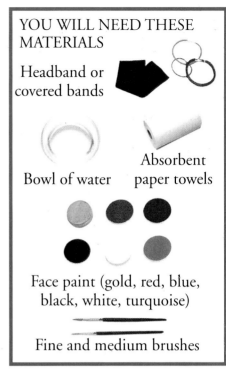

YOU WILL NEED THESE MATERIALS

Headband or covered bands

Bowl of water

Absorbent paper towels

Face paint (gold, red, blue, black, white, turquoise)

Fine and medium brushes

Handy hint

Gold face paint is a bit more expensive than other colors. If you do not have gold face paint, use yellow instead.

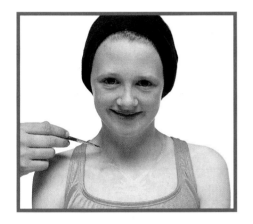

1 Tie the hair back. Paint the outlines of the necklace in gold face paint using a medium brush. Do two coats, if necessary.

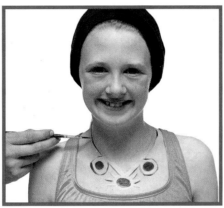

2 Fill in the outlines with red and blue face paints. Paint a thin black line around the necklace and pendants with a fine brush.

3 Paint a gold band around the wrist, then paint the outline for the watch face and straps black. Use the fine brush to paint the watch face white and the clock hands turquoise.

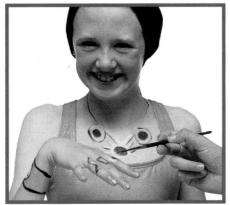

4 Use a clean fine brush to paint the gold outlines of rings onto the fingers. Allow to dry before painting exquisite turquoise, ruby and sapphire gems onto the rings.

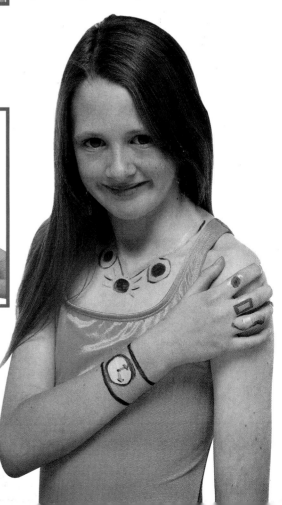

Soccer Hero

You do not have to buy your soccer team's uniform—you can paint it on! Body painting is lots of fun, especially when the paint is being applied to ticklish spots. Try not to laugh too much or you will end up with socks covered with wiggly lines. Remove body paint under the shower and dry yourself with an old towel.

YOU WILL NEED THESE MATERIALS

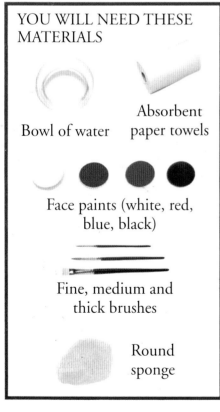

Bowl of water

Absorbent paper towels

Face paints (white, red, blue, black)

Fine, medium and thick brushes

Round sponge

When painting the feet, apply paint only to the tops and sides. Black footprints all over the carpet might not be appreciated.

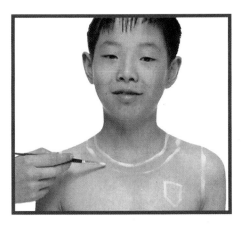

1 Make an outline on the chest and back in white face paint for the front and the back of the soccer shirt. This is best done with a medium or thick brush. Do not forget to paint the outline of the team's badge.

2 Use the thick brush to paint broad red lines inside the white outlines. Paint a red line around the waist. In white face paint, go over the outline to make the collar. Paint the sleeves white with a thick brush.

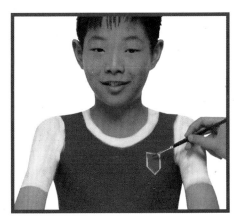

3 Use the round sponge to paint the rest of the shirt. To make the face paint go on easily, slightly moisten the sponge before applying the face paint. Paint the details on the badge using a fine brush.

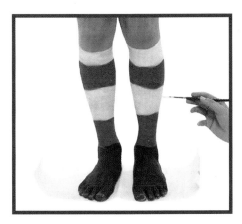

4 Wash the sponge thoroughly and cover the floor with absorbent paper towels. Paint the tops of the feet black using the clean sponge. Use a thick brush to paint red and white bands around both legs.

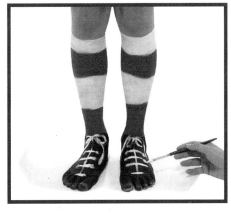

5 Stand as still as you can while the black paint dries. When it is dry, paint on white boot laces with a medium or thick brush. To make the laces show up, apply the white face paint thickly.

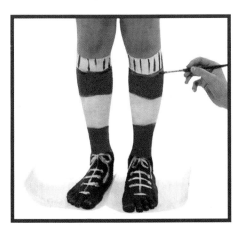

6 Paint short black lines onto the top bands with a medium brush. Then paint a black line around each leg for the sock turnovers. The paint must be dry before the soccer hero can kick the ball and score the winning goal.

Digital Soccer

Get your friends together and paint each other's hands in soccer uniforms. To play Digital Soccer, divide into two teams and move the ball around a tabletop field. Use your fingers to kick the ball into goal. "Head" the ball by bouncing it off the back of your hands.

YOU WILL NEED THESE MATERIALS

Triangular sponge Dishcloth

Ping-Pong ball Face paints (red, white, black)

2 medium brushes Acrylic paint (black, white)

1 Lay the dishcloth on your work surface. Apply a base coat of white face paint to one or both hands with a triangular sponge. Allow to dry.

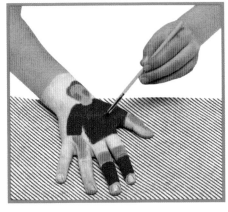

2 Paint the red socks and shirt with the medium brush. Paint the face, arms and knees in a skin tone color. Allow to dry for a few minutes.

3 Paint a black outline around the player. Now you can paint in his black boots and facial features.

4 Paint a Ping-Pong ball with black acrylic paint. When the paint has dried, carefully add the white markings you find on a soccer ball. World Cup Digital Soccer, here we come!

To make the playing field, cover a tabletop with newspaper or a large sheet of paper and use a felt-tip pen to mark the lines. Cut one long-side end off each of two small boxes to make the goals. It does not matter what size the boxes are as long as they are exactly the same size. Attach a goal at each end of the field using double-sided tape. You are now ready to kick off!

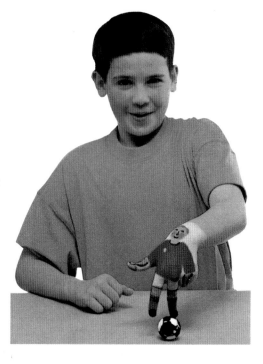

Little Devil

We can use our hands and fingers to make all sorts of shapes and creatures, including this Little Devil. Face paints, a cape and a fork complete the illusion. The first and fourth fingers form the devil's horns. The two middle fingers curl over to make the hair.

YOU WILL NEED THESE MATERIALS

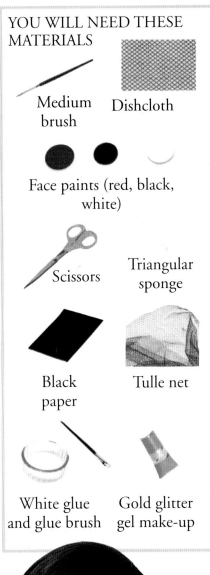

Medium brush

Dishcloth

Face paints (red, black, white)

Scissors

Triangular sponge

Black paper

Tulle net

White glue and glue brush

Gold glitter gel make-up

1 Lay down a dishcloth. Sponge the palm and back of the hand, wrist and thumb red. Paint the first finger and little finger white and the two middle fingers black with the brush.

2 When dry, paint the tip of the thumb and the base of the little finger black. Paint Little Devil's face and beard black using the medium brush. Outline the teeth with black and fill in with white face paint.

3 Use a finger to gently smear gold glitter gel make-up over the red paint on the wrist. This will make Little Devil's neck glint and shimmer.

To finish, cut a length of red tulle net and tie it around the wrist. Cut out a pitchfork from black paper and glue it to the front of the cape.

Alien from Outer Space

Aliens can come in many different forms. This extraterrestrial beauty is the famous many-eyed creature from the planet Agog. This alien sees everything. Even when asleep, the extra pair of eyes on its eyelids keep a watchful gaze. Just to be certain it misses nothing, there is a pair of cardboard eyes on straws attached to a headband. Double creepy!

YOU WILL NEED THESE MATERIALS

Headband or covered bands

Bowl of water

Absorbent paper towels

Face paints (green, white, blue, black, red)

Fine and thick brushes

This alien is green, but you could choose to be a red, blue, purple or yellow life-form. Try to think up an imaginative name for your home planet.

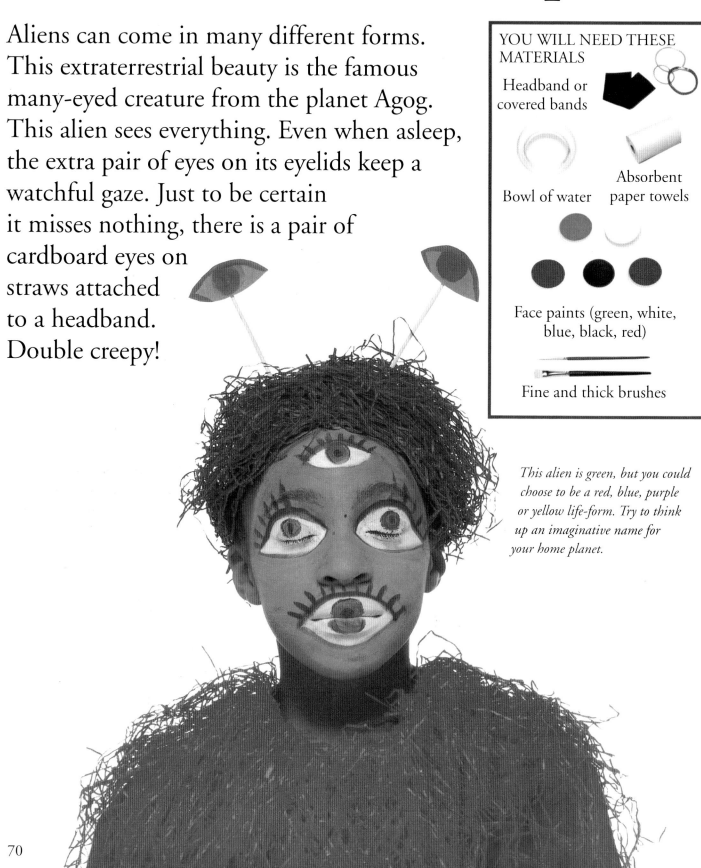

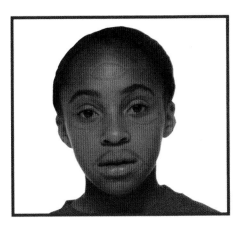

1 Tie the hair back. Use the fine brush to paint the outlines of four oval eye shapes in green face paint. You will need to close your eyes and mouth while the outlines are being painted.

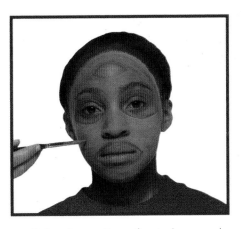

2 Paint the outline of a circle around the face in green face paint with the thick brush. Do two coats, if necessary. Fill in the outline with green. Clean and dry the thick brush thoroughly.

3 When the green face paint is dry, fill in the four eye shapes with white face paint. Do this with the clean thick brush. Apply the paint thickly and do two coats, if necessary.

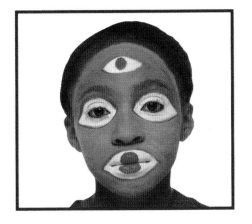

4 Allow the white face paint to dry thoroughly. Then paint blue circles onto the eyes on the lips and forehead. These are the irises of the eyes. Apply two coats if necessary.

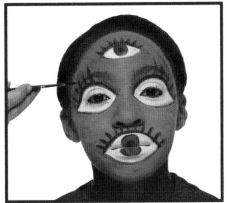

5 When the blue face paint is dry, paint a black dot onto the irises to make the pupils. Use the fine brush to paint a red line above the eyes and to make the eyelashes.

6 Close your eyes and stay very still while the irises are painted blue. When the paint is dry, paint on black pupils. Watch out! The many-eyed alien has arrived.

Alien costume

The planet Agog is covered with multicolored raffia and so are its inhabitants. Raffia is wound around their heads and used to form a cape over their shoulders. But do you know what is under the cape? More pairs of eyes, of course. When you make a pair of eyes to wear on your head, cut out and color extra pairs and stick them to your T-shirt with double-sided tape. When you open your raffia cape to reveal the secret eyes, your friends will be agog!

To fasten the cardboard eyes to plastic straws, use tape. To get them to stick on your head, bend the bottom of the straws and push them under a headband. If they wobble around, attach them to the headband with more tape.

The Vampire

When it comes to being truly scary, vampires know all the tricks. They dress in black and only come out at night. Their faces are a fright. Who else would dare to be seen with drooling fangs and red-rimmed eyes?

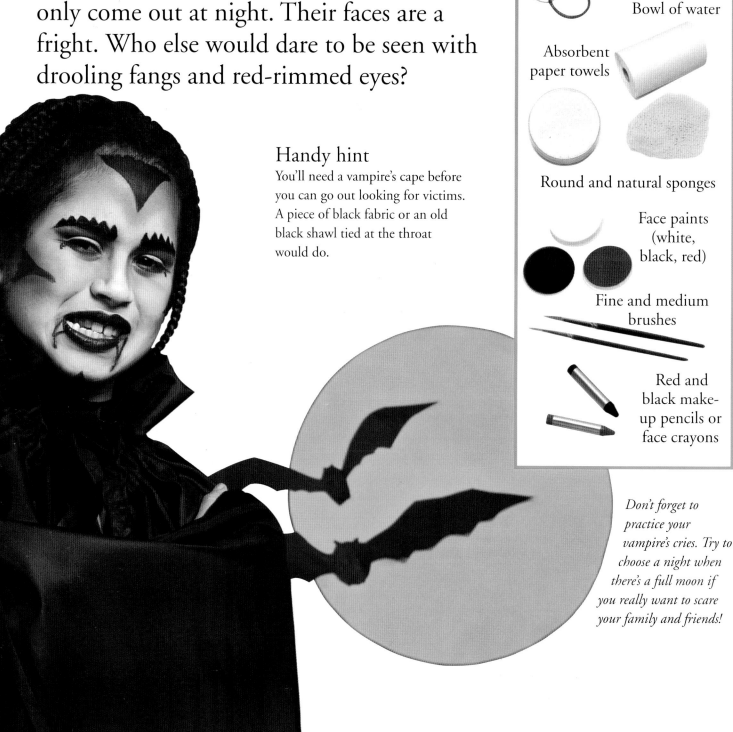

Handy hint
You'll need a vampire's cape before you can go out looking for victims. A piece of black fabric or an old black shawl tied at the throat would do.

YOU WILL NEED THESE MATERIALS
Headband or hair elastics

Bowl of water

Absorbent paper towels

Round and natural sponges

Face paints (white, black, red)

Fine and medium brushes

Red and black make-up pencils or face crayons

Don't forget to practice your vampire's cries. Try to choose a night when there's a full moon if you really want to scare your family and friends!

1 Tie the hair back so no loose strands touch the face. Slightly moisten the round sponge. Apply a light coat of white face paint, being careful not to get any in the mouth and eyes. The face paint should cover the whole face and reach below the jawline.

2 Using the fine brush, draw an outline in black face paint for the dark triangular area on the forehead. Carefully fill this area in with black using the medium brush. Now repeat this process for the triangular areas on the chin and cheeks.

3 Wait a few minutes for the triangular areas to dry thoroughly. Next, use the fine brush to paint the heavy eyebrows in black face paint. Let these dry. If necessary, add a second coat of paint so that the eyebrows look heavy and menacing.

4 Paint a thick white line on both eyelids. When dry, use the natural sponge to dab black shadows below the eyebrows and around the jawline and forehead. Carefully draw a red line under the eyes.

5 Color the lips with a black make-up pencil or face crayon. The vampire should smile while this is being done so that the color goes on smoothly. But not for long, as a vampire cannot be seen looking too friendly.

6 Outline the drooling fangs with black face paint using the fine brush. Now for the final gory touch. Use a clean brush to dab a little red face paint on the ends of the fangs and just below the eyes. Gross!

Craft tips

The face paints should be used boldly to get a really dramatic effect. You should also try to keep as still as you possibly can while your face is being painted. If you feel the temptation to giggle or scratch, close your eyes and concentrate on not moving.

Snazzy Glasses

These glasses are simple to paint and they are perfect if you do not like to wear lots of face paint. These fake glasses also let you play a great joke on your friends. When you have worn the Snazzy Glasses, create some eye-boggling designs of your own.

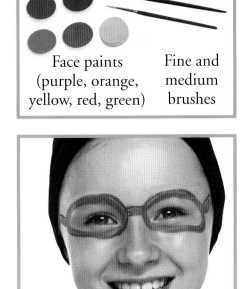

YOU WILL NEED THESE MATERIALS AND TOOLS

Headband or hair elastics

Bowl of water and absorbent paper towels

Face paints (purple, orange, yellow, red, green)

Fine and medium brushes

1 Tie the hair back. Paint the outline of the glasses in purple face paint with the fine brush. Let dry. Then do a second coat.

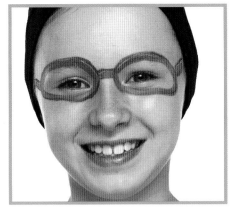

2 Make the glasses frames thicker by painting an orange line inside the purple outline. Do this with the medium brush.

3 Use the medium brush to paint the yellow wings on the frames. The wings can be whatever shape you want: zig-zag, curvy or straight.

4 To make the crazy wings on the glasses really stand out, outline them with purple face paint. Use the fine brush for this. Two coats will achieve a more dramatic effect.

5 For a really wacky look, paint a purple and red flower on one cheek. Paint some green leaves around the flower and paint the lips red.

74

Spooky Skeleton

This skeleton is great for Halloween trick or treating. The face and body painting is so convincing, it is chillingly scary. Turn the lights out and all your friends will be able to see is the outline of your "bones." Truly terrifying!

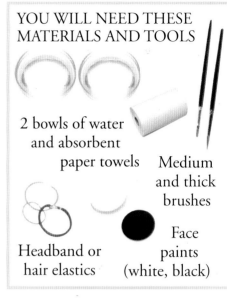
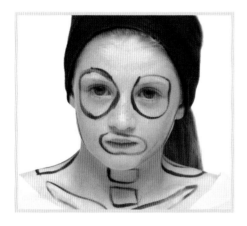

1 Dress the skeleton model in Halloween costume. Tie the hair back and cover the costume with paper towels. Paint black outlines, with a medium brush.

2 Fill in the outlines with black face paint using the thick brush. Do two coats. Let the paint dry before starting the next step.

3 Wash the brush thoroughly. Carefully fill in all the unpainted areas with white face paint using the thick brush.

4 Let the face paint dry. Using the medium brush, paint a black triangle down each side of the nose. Let them dry before applying a second coat of black paint.

5 Use the medium brush to paint black lines over the lips. These are the skeleton's teeth. Paint on a second coat to make the teeth really stand out. Now it is time to rattle those bones!

Munching Mouse

Mice are famous nibblers, so this field mouse has a pair of big front teeth. To play the part of a mouse you must twitch your nose, have startled-looking eyes, scuttle around quickly and quietly and nibble on a chunk of cheese. Practice these mousy actions and you will soon have your friends and family clambering onto chairs!

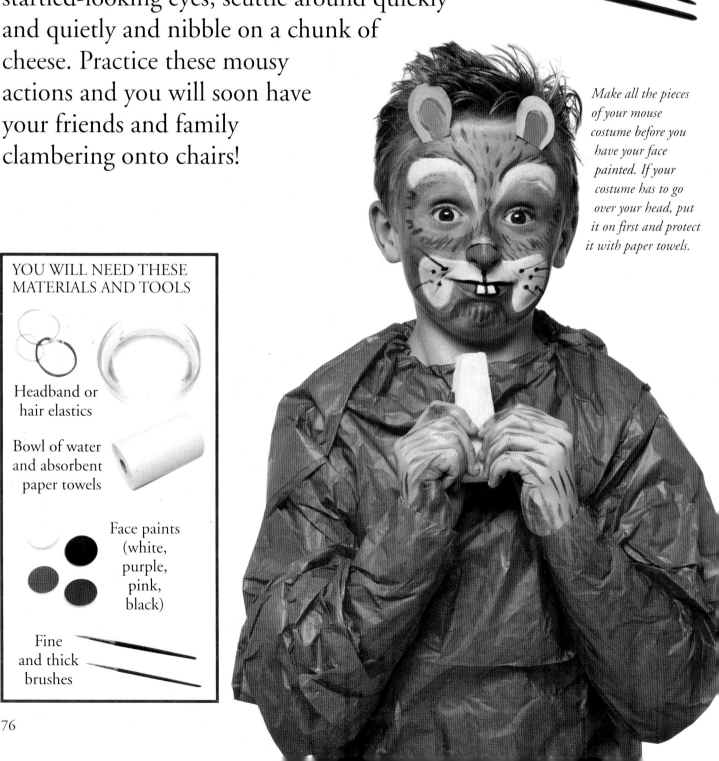

Make all the pieces of your mouse costume before you have your face painted. If your costume has to go over your head, put it on first and protect it with paper towels.

YOU WILL NEED THESE MATERIALS AND TOOLS

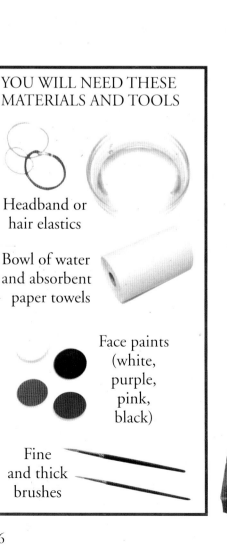

Headband or hair elastics

Bowl of water and absorbent paper towels

Face paints (white, purple, pink, black)

Fine and thick brushes

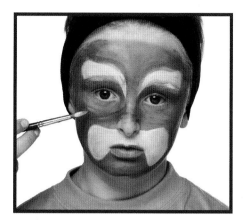

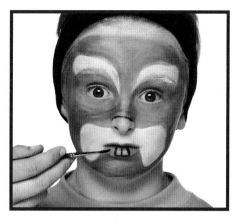

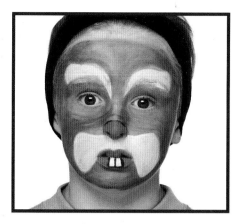

1 Tie the hair back. Paint in white eyebrows and cheeks with the thick brush. Next, apply the purple face paint with the thick brush, as shown above. The purple face paint should extend below the chin. Do not color in the tip of the mouse's nose.

2 Use the fine brush to paint a black line over the nose below the bridge. Making sure that the mouse's mouth is closed, paint black outlines for the teeth on the lower lip. The mouse must not laugh while this is being done! Wait a few minutes while the outlines dry.

3 Fill in the teeth with white paint. Next, paint the nose below the black line pink. When the teeth have dried completely, use the fine brush to paint the rest of the lips pink. This needs to be done very carefully so that the teeth are not smudged.

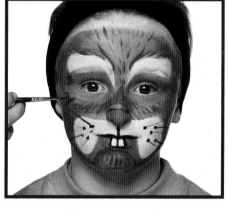

4 Paint some small black dots on the white area on either side of the nose, using the tip of the fine brush. Paint a black whisker sprouting out from each of the dots.

5 Mix a little black face paint into the purple to make a dark purple. Use this to paint the mouse's fur. The best way to do this is to make short, quick strokes with the fine brush.

Munching Mouse costume

Make your mouse's costume from pink or purple tissue paper or satin fabric. You could add a tail and sew or paint claws onto old gloves or mittens. Make a pair of mouse ears out of cardboard or fabric. Put a little gel in your hair for a really ratty look. Lastly, do not forget a piece of foam, fabric—or real—cheese to nibble!

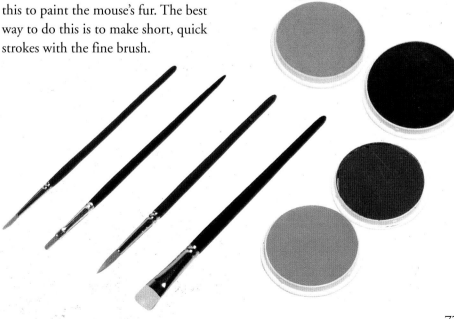

T-shirt
Painting

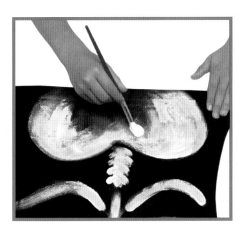

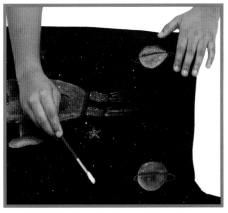

Petra Boase

Introduction

This puppy T-shirt has a surprise on the back—it is covered in muddy paw prints!

Decorating T-shirts with fabric paints and material is fun and very easy to do. In no time at all you will be creating stylish and wacky T-shirts for yourself, friends and family.

This section shows you how to prepare the T-shirts for painting as well as how to use different types of fabric paints to achieve stunning effects. It is also bursting with ideas. There are T-shirt designs for sports fans, animal lovers and aspiring astronauts. There is even a T-shirt design for bug collectors—this one will give you goosebumps!

Many of these designs can be used for a costume or for school plays. All you need to complete the outfits are leggings or shorts, a hat and a bit of face painting.

Most of the projects are simple to do. A few are more difficult and use special techniques. If you have never done any fabric painting before, it might be a good idea to start on one of the easier projects, like Basketballer.

The colors and types of fabric paints used in the designs are only suggestions. Change them to create different effects and to suit the clothes you will be wearing with the T-shirt. The ultimate design is really up to you. You should feel free to modify patterns and to come up with your own ideas.

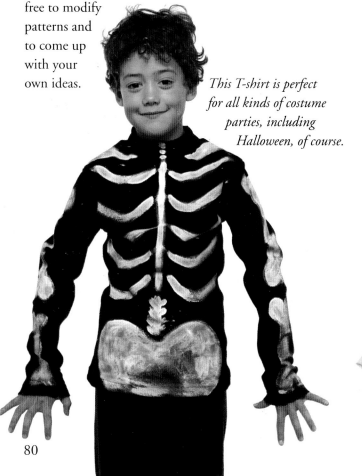

This T-shirt is perfect for all kinds of costume parties, including Halloween, of course.

Safety

❖ Always keep fabric paints and sharp utensils out of the reach of small children.

❖ Read the instructions on fabric paint packaging before you start painting. Follow the manufacturer's guidelines for preparing the T-shirt, mixing and applying paints and for drying wet paint. Some manufacturers will also recommend washing or ironing the painted T-shirt before wearing it.

❖ Ask an adult to iron the T-shirt and to supervise the use of sharp tools.

❖ If you splash fabric paint on your clothes, soak them immediately in lots of cold water. Keep rinsing the garments until the fabric paint is removed. Then, wash the clothes in warm, soapy water.

This T-shirt is also a game of Tic-tac-toe. Play it on long journeys—or whenever you're feeling bored.

Materials and Tools

These are the materials and tools you will need to complete the projects that follow.

Cardboard Large pieces of cardboard are inserted into the body and sleeves of a T-shirt to keep wet fabric paint from seeping through. You can buy sheets of thick cardboard or use cardboard from recycled packaging and boxes.

Chalk fabric marker This is a special white chalk that is used for drawing outlines onto dark-colored T-shirts.

Fabric glitter This is special glitter that can be attached to fabric with fabric glue. It is very fine, so use it carefully.

Fabric glue This glue will stick pieces of fabric together. Always use a special brush for applying fabric glue.

Fabric marker pen A fabric marker pen looks like a normal felt-tip pen, but it is designed to be used on fabric.

Fabric paint Fabric paint is applied to fabric and will not wash out. Read the instructions on the container before using it.

Fluorescent fabric paint Under ultraviolet light, this paint will glow. It comes in many bright colors.

Glitter fabric paint This sparkly fabric paint comes in a tube or squeeze bottle. Always read the instructions on the packaging before using glitter fabric paint.

Hair dryer You will need a hair dryer with a low heat setting to dry puffy fabric paint. Ask permission before using a hair dryer.

Pearlized or iridescent fabric paint This fabric paint dries with a special sheen. It comes in a squeeze bottle.

Puffy fabric paint When dried with a hair dryer, this paint puffs up. It comes in a squeeze bottle. Always follow the manufacturer's instructions when using puffy fabric paint.

Sponge You can buy an inexpensive sponge at a drug store. A sponge dipped in fabric paint and gently pressed onto fabric makes an interesting texture.

Sticky-back Velcro dots These dots stick to each other when pressed together.

T-shirt For the projects you will need cotton T-shirts. There are designs for short-sleeved and long-sleeved styles.

Sponge

Water pot

Puffy fabric paint

Pearlized fabric paint

Glitter fabric paint

Cardboard

Embroidery needle

Embroidery floss

Paper

Thick paintbrush

Sewing needle and thread

Ruler

Fabric paints

Medium paintbrush

Tracing paper

Scissors

Fine paintbrush

Newspaper

Fabric marker pen

Sequins

Sticky-back Velcro dots

Sewing pins

T-shirt

Pencil

Fluorescent fabric paints

Glitter

Fabric glue and brush

Chalk fabric marker

Hair dryer

Ribbons

Felt

81

Getting Started

Before you can start painting, you must prepare the T-shirt and perfect your design. The more time you spend getting these things right, the more spectacular the results will be.

If you are using a new T-shirt, first wash it to remove excess dye. When the T-shirt is dry, ask an adult to iron it to smooth out creases.

To stop fabric paint from seeping through the T-shirt, insert pieces of cardboard into the body and sleeves. The pieces of cardboard should fit snugly into position.

Draw drafts of your design on a piece of paper before drawing it on the T-shirt. Fabric marker pen, like fabric paint, cannot be washed out.

When you are happy with your design, draw it onto the T-shirt. Use a fabric marker pen on light-colored T-shirts, and a chalk marker on dark T-shirts.

When you are ready to start painting and have gathered all the necessary materials and tools, you must cover the work surface with a large sheet of wipe-clean plastic or lots of sheets of newspaper. It is also a good idea to protect any nearby furniture. Fabric paint can splatter, especially if you are flicking a brush loaded with fabric paint to get a special effect. Protect your clothing with an apron and old shirt—fabric paint will not wash off.

Painting tips

Fabric paints come in many wonderful colors and textures, but it is not necessary for you to have everything to create stunning designs on a T-shirt.

Fabric paint colors, just like normal acrylic or poster paint colors, can be mixed to make other colors. This means, for example, that you can mix blue puffy fabric paint with yellow puffy fabric paint to make green puffy fabric paint. You can also mix glitter fabric paint colors to make other colors.

To make fabric paint colors lighter, add white fabric paint to the color or simply add a little water. Fabric paint colors can be made darker by adding a little black fabric paint.

How to mix colors: yellow + blue = green, yellow + red = orange, red + blue = purple.

Mix large batches of a color in a water pot or small bowl. Add a little water to paints to make them go further.

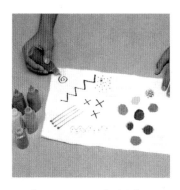

Before painting the T-shirt, try out the techniques and the colors on a piece of leftover fabric. This is especially important when using fabric paints in squeeze bottles.

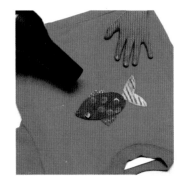

Puffy paint only puffs up when it is dried with a hair dryer set on low heat. Before drying other fabric paints with a hair dryer, check the instructions on the paint container.

Stencils and Templates

You will need to make stencils and templates to complete some of the T-shirts.

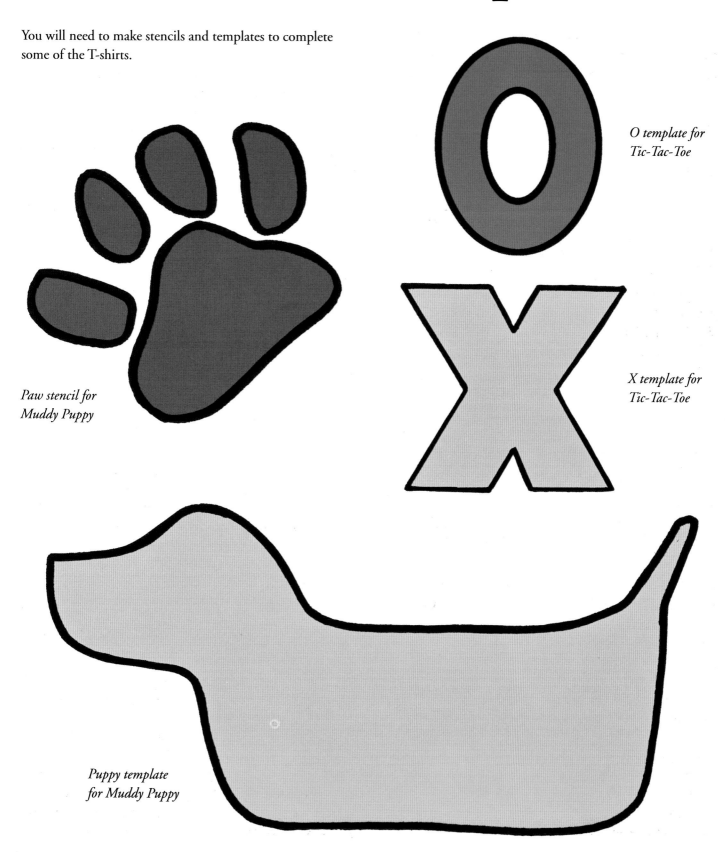

O template for Tic-Tac-Toe

X template for Tic-Tac-Toe

Paw stencil for Muddy Puppy

Puppy template for Muddy Puppy

Tic-Tac-Toe

This T-shirt is a lot of fun. Well, it is not often that an item of clothing doubles as a board game, is it? Wear it when you are traveling long distances and you will never be bored.

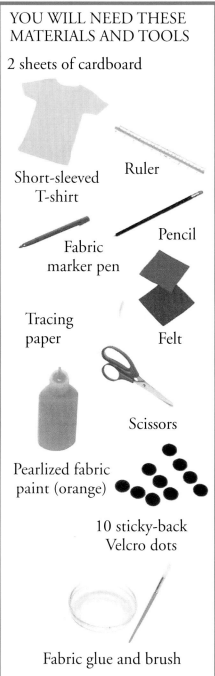

YOU WILL NEED THESE
MATERIALS AND TOOLS

2 sheets of cardboard

Short-sleeved
T-shirt

Ruler

Fabric
marker pen

Pencil

Tracing
paper

Felt

Scissors

Pearlized fabric
paint (orange)

10 sticky-back
Velcro dots

Fabric glue and brush

Three 0s in a row means that the boy has won this game of Tic-Tac-Toe.

84

1 Insert a piece of cardboard inside the body of the T-shirt. The cardboard should fit snugly. Use a ruler and fabric marker pen to measure and draw the Tic-Tac-Toe grid. The lines should be 9$^1/_2$ in long and 3 in apart.

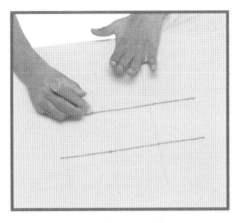

2 Go over the lines with orange pearlized fabric paint in a squeeze bottle. Move the tube evenly and smoothly along the lines—otherwise the pearl paint will form blobs. Allow the pearlized paint to dry thoroughly before continuing.

3 Trace and cut out the Tic-Tac-Toe templates in the Introduction. Place the templates on the felt and draw around them. You will need five red 0s and five blue Xs. Cut out the shapes. Also cut out five small blue ovals and glue these onto the 0s with fabric glue.

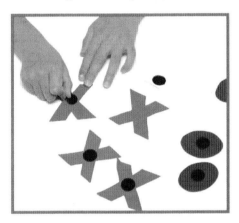

4 Remove the backing from the sticky side of a Velcro dot. Press the sticky surface onto the center of the back of one of the felt shapes. Repeat for all the remaining shapes.

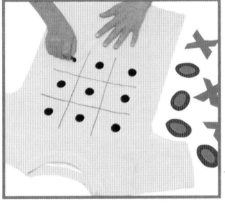

5 Remove the backing from the remaining dots and press them firmly onto the center of each square on the grid.

Do not forget to remove the 0s and Xs before washing the T-shirt.

6 You are now ready to play tic-tac-toe. Have fun!

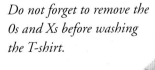

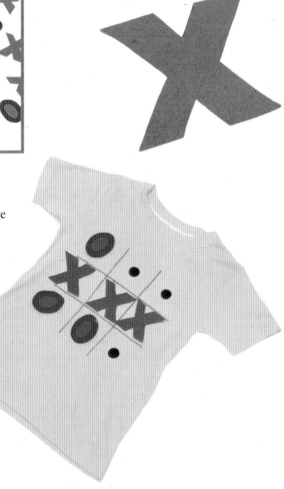

Basketballer

If you can slam dunk and dribble, then this is the T-shirt design for you. Why not get friends together to form a basketball team? You can each have a different number and choose your own team colors.

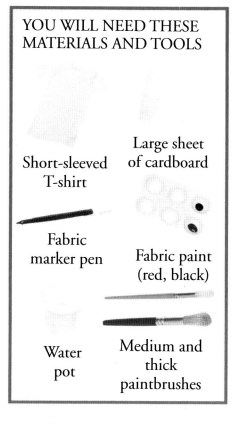

1 Insert cardboard inside the body and sleeves of the T-shirt. Use the fabric marker pen to outline the number 7 onto the front. Draw two bands along the edge of each sleeve front.

2 Use the thick brush to fill in the outline of the number and the bands on each sleeve with red fabric paint. Allow the paint to dry. Use the medium brush to paint a black line around the number and above the red band on the sleeve.

To make your T-shirt look professional, use a ruler when drawing the outlines of the number.

3 Paint the ribbing around the neck of the T-shirt with black fabric paint. When dry, use the medium brush to paint the narrow red line. Allow to dry. Turn over the T-shirt and repeat steps 1, 2 and 3.

Skeleton

This T-shirt is perfect for a costume party. All you need to complete your nightmare outfit is a black cap, black leggings and a pair of black gloves. Make up your face with white face paint and black eye shadow.

YOU WILL NEED THESE MATERIALS AND TOOLS

Long-sleeved black T-shirt

Large sheet of cardboard

Chalk fabric marker

Fabric paint (white)

Thick paintbrush

Water pot

1 Insert cardboard inside the T-shirt body and sleeves. Use the chalk fabric marker to draw outlines of the shoulder blades, rib cage, spine and hips onto the front of the T-shirt. Draw outlines of the arm bones onto both sleeves.

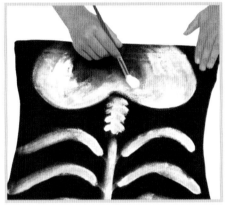

2 Use the thick brush to paint the bones on the front of the T-shirt with white fabric paint. To make the bones really white, do two coats. Allow the paint to dry between coats.

To repeat this design onto the back, allow the T-shirt to dry, then turn it over and repeat steps 1, 2 and 3.

3 To finish, paint the bones on both sleeves. Let the white fabric paint dry thoroughly between coats. All you have to do now, as a Skeleton, is to wait for a full moon!

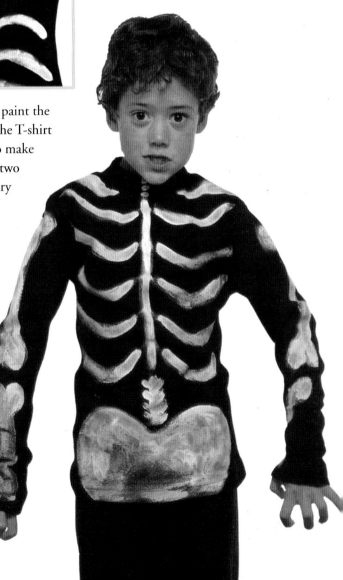

Space Trekker

This T-shirt goes where no other T-shirt has gone before. Its glowing fluorescent yellow afterburners will be seen by alien beings in every far-flung galaxy and planet. But all Space Trekkers should make sure that they know how to get back to planet earth!

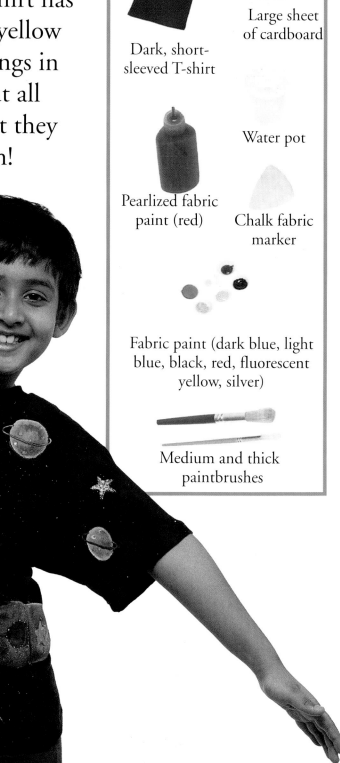

YOU WILL NEED THESE MATERIALS AND TOOLS

Dark, short-sleeved T-shirt

Large sheet of cardboard

Pearlized fabric paint (red)

Water pot

Chalk fabric marker

Fabric paint (dark blue, light blue, black, red, fluorescent yellow, silver)

Medium and thick paintbrushes

This earth-bound Space Trekker dreams of blasting off in his rocket and crashing through the earth's atmosphere. He wants to discover the secrets of the solar system and find out about life on other planets.

1 Insert cardboard inside the body and sleeves of the T-shirt. Use the chalk fabric marker to outline the planets, stars and rocket. Draw only the end of the rocket onto the front of the T-shirt.

2 Use the medium and thick brushes to paint the rocket with dark blue, light blue, black and red fabric paint. Use fluorescent yellow fabric paint for the rivets and afterburners. Paint the top of the rocket silver.

3 Paint the stars with silver fabric paint. Use plain and fluorescent fabric paints for the planets. When dry, make a ring around each planet with red pearlized fabric paint. Use the pearlized fabric paint to add details to the rocket.

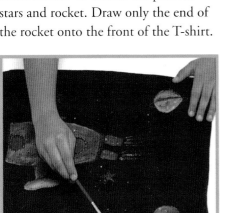

4 To make galaxies of stars, dip the thick brush in yellow fluorescent fabric paint and then flick the brush at the T-shirt. Allow to dry.

5 Turn the T-shirt over. Use the chalk fabric marker to draw the nose of the rocket to line up with the section on the front. Paint the rocket and stars as before.

Paint the solar system

Imagine how impressed your teacher would be if you painted the solar system onto your Space Trekker T-shirt. You know that the earth looks like a green and blue ball from outer space, but do you know what the other eight planets look like? To find out about Mercury, Venus, Mars, Jupiter, Saturn, Uranus, Neptune and Pluto, find some pictures in a reference book.

Muddy Puppy

Oh, no! Someone has let the puppy walk all over this T-shirt with its muddy paws. Surely such a naughty puppy does not deserve to be given a big, juicy bone. To keep the puppy from covering everything with mud, it has been given a fancy pair of socks to wear.

This boy just cannot believe what the Muddy Puppy has done to his white T-shirt. To find out for yourself, look on the next page.

look on the next page.

YOU WILL NEED THESE
MATERIALS AND TOOLS

Short-sleeved
T-shirt

2 sheets
of cardboard

Scissors

Water pot

Fabric paint (brown, black, white, turquoise, red, pale blue, yellow)

Fine and thick
paintbrushes

Fabric
marker pen

Pencil

Fabric glue
and brush

Tracing paper

Sponge

Narrow yellow
ribbon

1 Insert cardboard inside the T-shirt body and sleeves. Trace the puppy template in the Introduction. Place the template on the front of the T-shirt. Draw around it with the fabric marker pen.

2 Paint the dog brown using the thick brush. If you do not have brown paint, make some by mixing blue, red and yellow. Allow to dry before starting the next step.

3 Use the fine brush to paint black spots onto the body. Continue using the black paint for the ear, tail, shoes and bone. Add features to the face and decorate the socks, shoes and collar.

4 When the paint is dry, tie the ribbon into a small bow. Attach the bow onto the collar with fabric glue. Hold the bow in position until the glue is dry.

5 Trace the paw print stencil in the Introduction. Cut out the stencil, as shown. Turn the T-shirt over, checking that the pieces of cardboard are still in position.

6 Hold the stencil on the T-shirt. Dab the stencil with brown fabric paint. Lift off the stencil. Repeat until the back of the T-shirt is covered with prints.

Stenciling is an easy way to create a repeating pattern. Look through magazines and books to find ideas for other stencils. You could use this same simple technique to cover a T-shirt with cars, flowers, airplanes, hearts, stars or even lots and lots of muddy puppies!

Bug Collector

Aargh! Do not look now but there are spiders and insects crawling all over you. The Bug Collector T-shirt is not for the squeamish—it is for the enthusiastic mini-beast collector who really wants to bug his friends and family. You can invent your own creatures or, better still, copy them from real life!

This is the perfect T-shirt to wear to a costume party. To make it even more horrifying, stick plastic spiders and other insects onto the T-shirt with double-sided tape. Do not forget to remove your eight- and six-legged plastic friends before you put the T-shirt in to be washed.

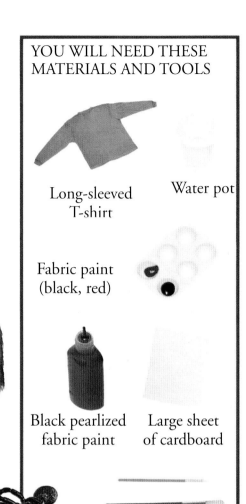

YOU WILL NEED THESE MATERIALS AND TOOLS

Long-sleeved
T-shirt

Water pot

Fabric paint
(black, red)

Black pearlized
fabric paint

Large sheet
of cardboard

Fine and medium
paintbrushes

Fabric marker pen

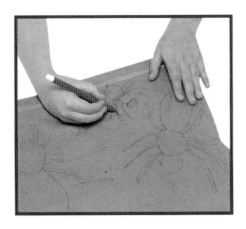

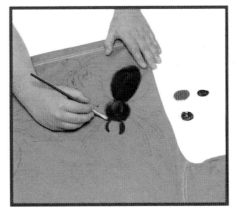

1 Insert pieces of cardboard inside the body and sleeves of the T-shirt. Use the fabric marker pen to draw two or three very large spiders onto the front of the T-shirt. Draw two or three spiders onto each sleeve.

2 Use the medium brush and black fabric paint to paint the spiders' heads, bodies and fangs. To paint the black jointed legs, use the fine brush. Wash the brush before painting the spiders' eyes red.

3 Dip a finger into black fabric paint and press it onto the T-shirt to make the body and head of a small insect. Repeat until you have covered the front and sleeves of the T-shirt with mini-beasts. Allow to dry.

4 To paint legs on the small bugs, use black pearlized fabric paint in a squeeze bottle. Allow the paint to dry thoroughly. If you want to, you can paint more spiders and bugs onto the back of the T-shirt.

Potato stamp mini-beasts

To make repeated designs, like small spiders or insects, you can make a stamp with a halved potato. Etch the outline of an insect's body into a cut surface of the potato with a blunt pencil. Ask an adult to cut away the potato from around the shape with a sharp knife. Dip the stamp lightly into fabric paint and press it onto the T-shirt. Keep stamping until you have covered your T-shirt. Paint the legs using black pearlized fabric paint. When dry, this paint has a raised and textured finish.

Index

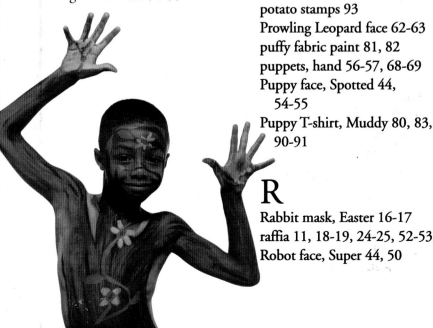

Acknowledgments

The publishers would like to thank the following children for appearing in this book, and of course their parents: Nana Addae, Richard Addae, Mohammed Adil Ali Ahmed, Josie and Lawrence Ainscombe, Clive Allen, Deborah Amoah, Charlie Anderson, Lauren Andrews, Rosie Anness, Michael Apeagyei, Tania Steve Aristizabal, Joshua Ashford, Emily Askew, Rula Awad, Nadia el-Ayadi, Joshua Ayshford, Nichola Barnard, Venetia Barrett, Jason Bear, Michael Bewley, Gurjit Kaur Bilkhu, Vikramjit Singh Bilkhu, Maria Bloodworth, Leah Bone, Catherine Brown, Chris Brown, Christopher Brown, Cerys Brunsdon, William Carabine, Daniel Carlow, Kristina Chase, Chan Chuvinh, Ngan Chuvinh, Alexander Clare, Rebecca Clee, Emma Cotton, Charlie Coulson, Brooke Crane, Charley Crittenden, Lawrence Defraitus, Dean Denning, Vicky Dummigan, Kimberley Durrance, Holly Everett, Alaba Fashina, Benjamin Ferguson, Terri Ferguson, Aimee Fermor, Kirsty and Rebecca Fraser, Fiona Fulton, Nicola Game, George Georgiev, Alice Granville, Lana Green, Liam and Lorenzo Green, Sophia Groome, Alexandra and Oliver Hall, Reece Harle, Laura Harris-Stewart, Jonathan Headon, Dominic Henry, Edward and Thomas Hogarth, Lauren Celeste Hooper, Mitzi Johanna Hooper, Sasha Howarth, Briony Irwin, Kayode Irwin, Gerald Ishiekwene, Saadia Jacobs, Stella-Rae James, Isha Janneh, Jade Jeffries, Aribibia Johnson, Rean Johnson, Reece Johnson, Carl Keating, Karina Kelly, Sarah Kenna, Camille Kenny-Ryder, Lee Knight, Nicola Kreinczes, Kevin Lake, Victoria Lebedeva, Barry Lee, Kirsty Lee, Isaac John Lewis, Nicholas Lie, Sophie, Alex and Otis Lindblom-Smith, Chloe Lipton, Scott Longstaff, Ephram Lovemore, Claire McCarthy, Erin McCarthy, Jock Maitland, Gabriella and Izabella Malewska, Ilaira and Joshua Mallalieu, Elouisa Markham, Alexander Martin-Simons, Laura Masters, Hou Mau, Trevor Meechan, Mickey Melaku, Imran Miah, Yew-Hong Mo, Kerry Morgan, Jessica and Alice Moxley, Aiden Mulcahy, Fiona Mulcahy, Tania Murphy, Moriam Mustapha, Lucy Nightingale, Ify Obi, Adenike Odeleye, Wura Odurinde, Laurence Ody, Folake Ogundeyin, Abayomi Ojo, Fola Oladimeji, Ola Olawe, Lucy Oliver, Michael Oloyede, Yemisi Omolewa, Tope Oni, Alexander and Dominic Paneth, Kim Peterson, Mai-Anh Peterson, Patrice Picard, Alice Purton, Josephina Quayson, Pedro Henrique Queiroz, Brandon Rayment, Alexandra Richards, Leigh Richards, Jamie Rosso, Nida Sayeed, Alex Simons, Charlie Simpson, Aaron Singh, Antonino Sipiano, Justine Spiers, Marlon Stewart, Tom Swaine Jameson, Catherine Tolstoy, Maria Tsang, Nicola and Sarah Twiner, Frankie David Viner, Sophie Louise Viner, Nhat Han Vong, Rupert and Roxy Walton, Devika Webb, George Wheeler, Claudius Wilson, Andreas Wiseman. Kate Yudt, Tanyel Yusef.

Contributors: Petra Boase, Stephanie Donaldson, Sarah Maxwell, Hugh Nightingale, Michael Purton, Thomasina Smith, Jacki Wadeson, Sally Walton.
Gratitude also to Hampden Gurney School, Walnut Tree Walk Primary School and St John the Baptist C. of E. School.

The authors would like to thank the following for their assistance in providing materials and advice—Boots; Dylon Consumer Advice; Head Gardener, Knightsbridge; Lady Jayne; Mason Pearson, Kent; Molton Brown; Tesco. Special thanks to Justin of Air Circus; 'Smiley Face' from Theatre Crew, Tunbridge Wells; and the Bristol Juggling Convention.